Lorraine Xmas, 1998
From Henning

Trees and Shrubs

of

Mandy
FSJ
09/26/2015

Kathleen Wilkinson

Illustrations by Joan Williams
Principle Photography by
Blaine Andrusek
Cliff Wallis
Cleve Wershler

First printed 1990 5 4 3 2

The Publisher:
Lone Pine Publishing
#206 10426-81 Avenue
Edmonton, Alberta, Canada
T6E 1X5

Canadian Cataloguing in Publication Data
Wilkinson, Kathleen, 1950-
      A habitat field guide to trees and shrubs of Alberta
      Bibliography: p.
      Includes index.
      ISBN 0-919433-39-1
      1. Trees — Alberta — Identification. 2. Shrubs
— Alberta — Identification. 3. Ecology — Alberta.
I. Title.
QK203.A5W54 1989 582.16097123 C88-091601-X

Cover Design: Yuet Chan
Cover Photo: Cleve Wershler
Typesetting: Personal Publishing
Printing: Kyodo Printing Co. (S'pore) Pte. Ltd., Singapore

The author gratefully acknowledges the assistance of the Recreation, Parks and Wildlife Foundation in funding the preparation of this manuscript.

The publisher gratefully acknowledges the assistance of the Federal Department of Communications, Alberta Culture and Multiculturalism, the Canada Council, the Recreation, Parks and Wildlife Foundation, and the Alberta Foundation for the Literary Arts in the publication of this book.

Dedicated to Helen Lloyd, former botany laboratory demonstrator at the University of Manitoba, and Beryl Hallworth, former assistant curator of the herbarium at the University of Calgary. They initiated and nurtured my own interest in botany, and, with their dedication and enthusiasm, have provided inspiring role models.

Distribution of this copy of Trees and Shrubs of Alberta,
has been undertaken by the
Youth-In-Action program of the
Recreation, Parks and Wildlife Foundation of Alberta.

This book is one of several major works of natural history
including Wild Mammals of Western Canada, Grizzly Bears,
Animal Tracks of Western Canada, Wolves and The Wonder of
Canadian Birds which have previously been distributed to school
libraries by the Foundation.

The Foundation believes the subject and quality of this book
will contribute to our children's understanding of the fragile
beauty of all wildlife, and its habitat and will help to further the
objectives of the Foundation, which are:
to develop and maintain recreational programs,
services and facilities
to develop and maintain parks
to manage and conserve fish and wildlife

The Foundation acknowledges with gratitude the co-operation
and assistance provided by the Honorable Jim Dinning, Minister
of Education, and the Honorable Dr. Stephen West, Minister of
Recreation and Parks in making this project possible.

For further information regarding the Foundation, its work,
and how you can participate, contact:

The Executive Director
Recreation, Parks and Wildlife Foundation
#705, 10045 - 111 Street
Edmonton, Alberta
T5K 1K4
Telephone: (403) 482-6467

Table of Contents

Deciduous Trees and Shrubs 63

Preface

Although there are a number of excellent wildflower guidebooks for specific areas of Alberta, little attention has been paid to the many woody plants of our province. The purpose of this book, therefore, is to introduce the interested observer to our native or naturalized trees and shrubs, in a colourful, easy to use, handy-sized format. To enhance the book's value to the non-botanist, technical terms have been avoided wherever possible. Where it has been necessary to use botanical terminology, definitions are provided within the main text, or readers may refer either to a glossary provided in the back or to the illustrated terminology in the front of the book.

Seventy-seven species in twenty-two plant families are described and illustrated, with 180 colour photographs and, in several cases, with line drawings to highlight specific features. In a book of this size it is not possible to mention every species of tree and shrub that occurs in the province. For this reason, only the more common or distinctive members of large and difficult to differentiate groups, such as the willows, are described here. In addition, I have usually included only those shrubs which are more than 30 cm in height, or smaller plants easily recognized as shrubs because of their thick, woody stems. Shrubs less than 30 cm in height — small members of the heath family, for example — are often not readily recognized as shrubs by the casual observer, and will therefore be described in a second volume on wildflowers of Alberta.

Acknowledgements

I would like to thank the following people for their help with this project:

Joan Williams for her painstaking drawings; Blaine Andrusek, Cliff Wallis, Cleve Wershler, and others who supplied slides; Dr. Peter Achuff for technical review of the manuscript; Bonnie Smith and Dr. C.C. Chinnappa for access to the University of Calgary herbarium; Julie Hrapko for slides, technical review and access to the botanical files of the Provincial Museum of Alberta; Beryl Hallworth, Gail Harrison and Taryn Campbell for providing reference material; Phillip Kennedy who reviewed Latin and Greek derivatives; Dr. John G. Packer and the University of Toronto Press for permission to use the distribution maps from *Flora of Alberta* (Please note: The distribution maps on the following pages: 34, 38, 46, 64, 70, 72, 78, 84, 98, 108, 112, 116-124, 128, 146, 150, 180 have been modified with kind permission of Dr. Packer and U of T Press. I accept the responsibility for any errors which may have occured as a result.) Nancy Turner and the Royal British Columbia Museum for permission to use ethno-botanical information from *Food Plants of British Columbia Indians: Parts 1 and 2, Plants in British Columbia Indian Technology*, and the *Edible Wild Plants of Canada* Series; and lastly, Mary Walters Riskin and Robin Bovey for being encouraging and supportive editors.

Special thanks is directed to the Recreation, Parks and Wildlife Foundation of Edmonton. This book could not have been written without their generous financial support.

- Kathleen Wilkinson

Introduction

What is a tree? What is a shrub? Sometimes it's hard to tell the difference. In several cases plants may grow as trees in one part of the country and shrubs in another. For our purposes, a tree is a perennial plant with a single, thick (usually 5 cm or more in diameter) woody stem as contrasted to a shrub, which has two or more main woody stems arising from or near the ground. This book includes mainly trees and shrubs that are native to Alberta, with some that are naturalized: that is, not native to the province, but capable of growing and reproducing here without our help. Caragana and Tartarian honeysuckle are common examples of naturalized species.

Trees and shrubs can be classified as: (a) coniferous, if they are cone-bearing and have leaves (often needle-like) which usually remain on the tree throughout the year; or (b) deciduous, if their leaves change colour and drop off, usually in the fall.

Conifers (from the Latin for "cone-bearing") have their reproductive structures in male or female cones and the seeds are usually loosely attached to the cone scales rather than being enclosed by the ovary, as in deciduous plants. The male cones bear pollen which is usually carried by wind to fertilize the female cones. Conifers are often referred to as evergreens because most of them retain their green, needle-like leaves all year round. The one exception is the larches. Their needles turn a vibrant golden-orange colour (forming a strikingly beautiful display in the mountains and muskegs in the late summer), before dropping off at the end of the growing season.

Deciduous trees and shrubs, in contrast, usually have broad leaves that change colour and are shed in the fall. Their reproductive organs are generally flowers and the seeds are enclosed by the ovary, forming a fruit. Although some flowering plants are pollinated by wind, many are pollinated by insects which are attracted by the colour and aroma of the flowers.

Most plants have "complete flowers," meaning that each flower has both male and female organs. The flowers of some species, however, have only male or female organs. In some tree and shrub species, male and female organs can be found on the same plant (called monoecious), while on others they are on separate plants (called dioecious).

All plants (and animals as well) are identified scientifically by a universally accepted Latin, scientific name composed of two parts. The scientific name of western hemlock is *Tsuga heterophylla*. The first part, *Tsuga*, indicates the group (or genus; plural genera) of related plants known as hemlocks. The second part, *heterophylla*, is the species or specific name, and tells us that we are dealing with western hemlock. Each species has one scientific name and this name is used in all the countries of the world. Scientific names usually describe some aspect of the plant and often have very interesting origins. For example *Tsuga* is derived from the Japanese name for the native hemlocks of Japan, while *heterophylla* is Latin for leaves of different sizes or shapes, from the Greek *heteros* (different) and *phyllon* (leaf).

In addition to scientific names, popular names are listed for each species in the book. The most common ones are typed in upper case; those that may be less familiar to Albertans follow in lower case. The trees and shrubs are listed by families (groups of related genera) in the order in which they occur in most botanical texts for this area. This order allows species that are closely related (and thus, usually similar in appearance) to be placed together, a feature which will help in identification. Within each family, the genera and species are arranged in alphabetical order based on their scientific names.

Having identified a plant, it's interesting to learn something about it, something that gives it character and sets it apart from the other plants. How did it get its name? Is it edible? Does it have medicinal properties? Where is it found throughout the world? These questions are answered in a comments section below the plant's description. Most of the information in this section has been derived from other published works, and for those readers who would like to pursue these aspects further, a selected Bibliography may be found in the back of the book.

A word of CAUTION: Plants contain potent chemicals. What is safe for one person to eat or use, may be unsafe or even fatal for another. Do not eat *any* wild plant unless you are positive that you have identified it correctly as an edible species. Sample a very small amount at first and allow at least 24 hours to see if any adverse reaction occurs.

Do not attempt to treat yourself for any medical condition using wild plants. The medicinal uses, particularly by native peoples, of plants mentioned in this book have not all been verified and are included for historic interest only.

Everyone at one time or another experiences the joy of identifying a plant only to discover that it cannot possibly occur where you have found it. No matter how much it looks like a picture of sagebrush, if you've found it in a wet northern bog, it is not sagebrush. Most plants are found in specific habitats, although some plants may be found over a wide range of climatic, soil and moisture conditions.

Various concepts have been used to describe the habitats where plants or animals occur. In this book the province has been subdivided into four major habitat types or natural regions based upon climate and vegetation characteristics. These are Prairie, Aspen Parkland, Boreal Forest and Rocky Mountain. Their climatic conditions and characteristic plants are briefly described below. Vegetation descriptions refer to natural landscapes of the area and do not take into account changes produced by human activities such as cultivation.

PRAIRIE

The Prairie occupies the majority of the southern quarter of the province (see map on page 13) and is characterized by low annual rainfall, high winds and a frost-free period ranging from approximately 115 days in the warm, dry southeast to 90 days in the cooler, wetter, northern and western portions.

The dry, southeastern Prairies are dominated by short grasses and sage.

The southeastern section of the Prairie is the driest, hottest and has the least snow accumulation. Warm winter chinooks are frequent and are a major factor in prohibiting tree growth except in areas of higher moisture such as north-facing coulee slopes, and along streams and rivers. The landscape is flat to rolling and is covered primarily by blue grama grass, spear grasses and wheat grasses, with splashes of colour provided by yellow daisies, pink ball cactus and old man's whiskers, and the blues of wild flax and slender blue beard-tongue. Look for such drought-tolerant shrubs as sagebrush, rabbit brush and

The tree and shrub communities along Prairie rivers provide valuable cover for animals.

11

greasewood here. In shaded ravines are shrubs which require more moisture, such as buckbrush, wolf-willow, saskatoon, hawthorn and choke cherry.

To the west, cooler summer temperatures, deeper snow cover and more precipitation result in more luxuriant growth. Blue grama grass, cactus and sagebrush gradually disappear, to be replaced by lupines, sticky geranium, northern bedstraw and Canada goldenrod. On the western edge of the grassland, fescues and oat grasses become more dominant and more trees and shrubs such as poplar, choke cherry, currants and gooseberries appear. Gradually the increasing presence of groves of aspen poplar signifies the start of the Aspen Parkland.

ASPEN PARKLAND

To the north and west of the Prairie grasslands lies a region of intermingled prairie and aspen groves known as the Aspen Parkland. This region receives more precipitation, particularly during the summer months, has lower winter temperatures, fewer chinooks and longer snow cover than most of the adjacent prai-

Farther west, cooler summer temperatures and moister conditions result in more luxuriant growth. Here the prairie is mixed grassland, with trees only along streams and in other low-lying areas.

In the Aspen Parkland, groves of aspen are intermingled with open, grassy areas.

Potholes in the Aspen Parkland provide essential nesting sites for ducks and geese.

Natural Regions

Prairie
Aspen Parkland
Boreal Forest
Montane
Subalpine
Alpine

ries. It is transitional between the Prairie and Boreal Forest to the north; between Prairie and Rocky Mountain natural regions to the west.

There are groves of aspen with occasional balsam poplar, white spruce and paper birch. Shrubs such as saskatoon, buckbrush, roses, wolf willow, choke cherry and beaked hazelnut are common, while wild sarsaparilla, asters, goldenrod, wild vetch, Solomon's seal, pea vine, violets, fairy bells, tall mertensia and cow parsnip are frequent in the herbaceous understory.

The Boreal Forest, the largest natural region in Alberta, covers the entire northern half of the province. Much of it is mixedwood forests of coniferous and deciduous trees.

BOREAL FOREST

The Boreal Forest is the largest natural region in Alberta, covering the northern half of the province and extending southward in a wedge between the mountains in the west and Aspen Parkland to the east. The Boreal Forest is also the largest natural region in Canada, stretching in a wide band across the country from Newfoundland to British Columbia. Winters are cold and long due to the influence of Arctic air masses, and summers range from warm in the south to cool in more northerly areas. Most of the annual precipitation falls as rain in

Open jack pine forests are common in drier, sandy areas.

Black spruce muskeg is typical of Boreal Forest.

the summer, allowing trees to flourish. White spruce, aspen poplar and balsam fir are present throughout upland areas while black spruce, swamp or bog birch and balsam poplar are characteristic of more poorly drained sites. Lodgepole pine is common in the southwest, where the Boreal Forest is transitional with the Montane natural region. In dry, sandy areas in central and northeastern sections, look for jack pine, bearberry, blueberry and lichen communities. In wet, cold muskegs, black spruce and sphagnum moss are abundant, with lesser amounts of tamarack, dwarf birch, Labrador tea, marsh cinquefoil, buck-bean, bog rosemary and bog cranberry.

ROCKY MOUNTAINS

The Rocky Mountain natural region may be further subdivided into three zones. These are, in order of increasing altitude, Montane, Subalpine and Alpine.

Montane

The first of these, the Montane, occupies a small area of the province along lower elevation river valleys in the mountains and in patches in the western foothills. The Montane zone is drier and warmer than both the Subalpine and Alpine, due to the strong influence of Pacific air masses.

Forests tend to be open with trees interspersed with grassy areas. Douglas fir and limber pine are characteristic southwestern Montane

Limber pine is characteristic of the southern foothills Montane zone.

15

species but they are often less abundant than trees such as lodgepole pine, white spruce and aspen poplar. Shrubs such as junipers, Canada buffaloberry and shrubby cinquefoil may be locally common, with willows in moist locations along creeks and rivers.

North- and east-facing slopes are generally more moist and support tree growth while south- and west-facing slopes are generally grass-covered.

Reed grasses, hairy wild rye, hedysarum, showy aster, milk-vetch and veiny meadow rue are found in the shade of the trees while rough fescue, spear grasses, oat grasses, northern bedstraw, fleabanes, sages, old man's whiskers and cinquefoils are common in grassy patches. Low-lying areas are dominated by sedges and willows.

Aspen stands are characteristic of many Montane habitats.

The foothills, although primarily Montane, are transitional between Prairie, Aspen Parkland, Boreal Forest, and the Rocky Mountains, and may have plants characteristic of all four natural regions.

Subalpine

As elevation increases, the climate becomes cooler and wetter with higher snowfall. These conditions are highly suitable for the development of dense coniferous forests of white and Engelmann spruce, and subalpine fir. Shrub growth is sparse in the deep shade of the trees, and consists of such species as false azalea, Labrador tea, and occasional bracted honeysuckle, rock willow, bristly black currant and Canada buffaloberry. Feather-mosses, on the other hand, thrive in these moist, shady conditions and form a thick, soft carpet punctuated with grouseberry, arnicas, bronze-bells, bunchberry, wintergreens, and twinflower.

At higher elevations, Engelmann spruce replaces white spruce and subalpine fir becomes more frequent. In the upper regions of the Subalpine, higher winds and the high intensity of the sun's rays produce increased moisture stress and the tree cover thins out. Such high-altitude tree species as white-bark pine and alpine larch may

Forest cover is dense at lower elevations in the Subalpine zone.

appear in small numbers and, as the Subalpine zone grades into the Alpine, tree growth is reduced to scattered islands of stunted, bushy, wind-flagged Engelmann spruce and subalpine fir called krummholz.

Alpine

Above tree-line (the limit of contiguous tree cover) is the Alpine zone, where tree growth is limited to occasional krummholz islands. Winters are cold and summers are cool; even during July and August the temperature may dip below zero. In addition, soils are frequently low in nutrients. Although these conditions inhibit the growth of trees

The forest becomes more open and the trees are shorter at upper elevation in the Subalpine.

17

and tall shrubs, many herbaceous species are adapted to survive, even flourish, here.

Wide diversity of species is possible over short distances in response to differences in levels of snow accumulation, snow melt patterns, degree of protection from wind, drainage and soil development.

A moist Alpine meadow.

Where snow accumulation is high and the snow does not melt until late in the season, sedges predominate, often forming a dense, hummocky turf. Where snow accumulation is somewhat less, moist meadows support a wide array of colourful flowers including heathers, valerian, paintbrushes, louseworts, buttercups, veronica, groundsels and gentians. More well-drained, exposed areas are dominated by carpets of white mountain avens.

On exposed mountain tops, only the hardiest plants can survive.

At higher elevations where high intensity solar radiation, strong winds and the low moisture-holding capacity of the soils produce drought conditions during the short growing season, plant cover is limited to species which take shelter in crevices or have com-

Although the Alpine zone is generally treeless, scattered krummholz may occur.

pact, cushion-growth forms such as whitlow grasses, saxifrages, moss campion and mountain chickweed. At the highest elevations only hardy lichens can exist, forming isolated patches of colour on boulders and rubble.

How to Use This Guide for Field Identification

1. For deciduous plants, compare your live specimen with the photographs and drawings. Species that look alike tend to be closely related and will usually be found together in this book. When you find a match, proceed to Step 2. For conifers, work carefully through the keys provided to arrive at the correct coniferous genus. Where members of a specific genus are difficult to tell apart, keys are provided to the species level.

2. Next, read the description, paying particular attention to the size, flower, fruit, or cone details and location. If you are unsure of a term, check the glossary, or the illustrated terminology. Check the map. It is unlikely, but not impossible, to find plants well outside the illustrated range.

3. To find out about a plant for which you know the common or scientific name, check the index.

4. If this book has piqued your curiosity and you would like further information, consult the Selected Bibliography.

Symbols for Natural Regions

Prairie

Montane

Aspen Parkland

Subalpine

Boreal Forest

Alpine

Keys to Coniferous Species

Because many conifers, especially those in the same genus, tend to look alike and are often difficult to distinguish by comparing them to photos, keys have been provided to aid in their identification. These keys consist of opposite leads which are mutually exclusive. By following through the key, choosing the leads which best describe your specimen, you should arrive at a genus or species. If you arrive at a genus, turn to the key for that particular genus and repeat the procedure until you have arrived at a species. Then compare your specimen with the picture and description of the species in this book. If they do not appear to be the same, go back to the start of the key and try again.

Some readers will ask why there is no key provided for the deciduous trees and shrubs described in this book. There are two reasons. First, because of the number of deciduous trees and shrubs involved, a key would be unwieldy and complicated for the non-professional to use. Second, in contrast to the conifers, the deciduous trees and shrubs are more readily distinguished using the photographs and descriptions only.

Key to Coniferous Species

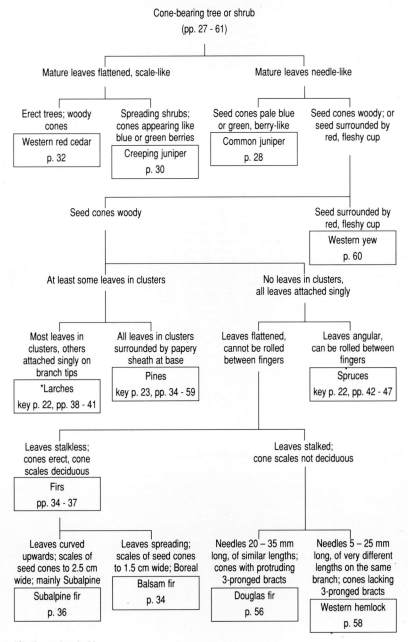

Cone-bearing tree or shrub
(pp. 27 - 61)

Mature leaves flattened, scale-like

Mature leaves needle-like

Erect trees; woody cones

Western red cedar
p. 32

Spreading shrubs; cones appearing like blue or green berries

Creeping juniper
p. 30

Seed cones pale blue or green, berry-like

Common juniper
p. 28

Seed cones woody; or seed surrounded by red, fleshy cup

Seed cones woody

Seed surrounded by red, fleshy cup

Western yew
p. 60

At least some leaves in clusters

No leaves in clusters, all leaves attached singly

Most leaves in clusters, others attached singly on branch tips

*Larches
key p. 22, pp. 38 - 41

All leaves in clusters surrounded by papery sheath at base

Pines
key p. 23, pp. 34 - 59

Leaves flattened, cannot be rolled between fingers

Leaves angular, can be rolled between fingers

Spruces
key p. 22, pp. 42 - 47

Leaves stalkless; cones erect, cone scales deciduous

Firs
pp. 34 - 37

Leaves stalked; cone scales not deciduous

Leaves curved upwards; scales of seed cones to 2.5 cm wide; mainly Subalpine

Subalpine fir
p. 36

Leaves spreading; scales of seed cones to 1.5 cm wide; Boreal

Balsam fir
p. 34

Needles 20 – 35 mm long, of similar lengths; cones with protruding 3-pronged bracts

Douglas fir
p. 56

Needles 5 – 25 mm long, of very different lengths on the same branch; cones lacking 3-pronged bracts

Western hemlock
p. 58

*Coniferous but deciduous

Key to the Larches

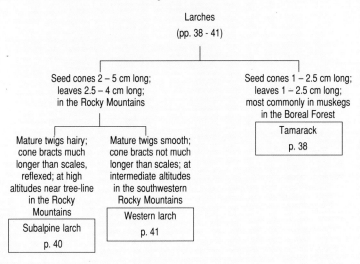

Larches
(pp. 38 - 41)

Seed cones 2 – 5 cm long;
leaves 2.5 – 4 cm long;
in the Rocky Mountains

Seed cones 1 – 2.5 cm long;
leaves 1 – 2.5 cm long;
most commonly in muskegs
in the Boreal Forest

Tamarack
p. 38

Mature twigs hairy;
cone bracts much
longer than scales,
reflexed; at high
altitudes near tree-line
in the Rocky
Mountains

Subalpine larch
p. 40

Mature twigs smooth;
cone bracts not much
longer than scales; at
intermediate altitudes
in the southwestern
Rocky Mountains

Western larch
p. 41

Key to the Spruces

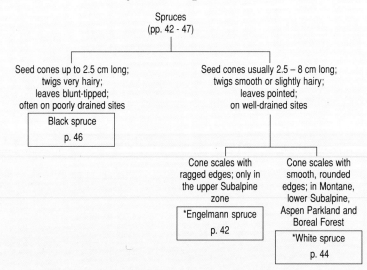

Spruces
(pp. 42 - 47)

Seed cones up to 2.5 cm long;
twigs very hairy;
leaves blunt-tipped;
often on poorly drained sites

Black spruce
p. 46

Seed cones usually 2.5 – 8 cm long;
twigs smooth or slightly hairy;
leaves pointed;
on well-drained sites

Cone scales with
ragged edges; only in
the upper Subalpine
zone

*Engelmann spruce
p. 42

Cone scales with
smooth, rounded
edges; in Montane,
lower Subalpine,
Aspen Parkland and
Boreal Forest

*White spruce
p. 44

*Engelmann and white spruce hybridize where their ranges overlap in the mountains and foothills.

Key to the Pines

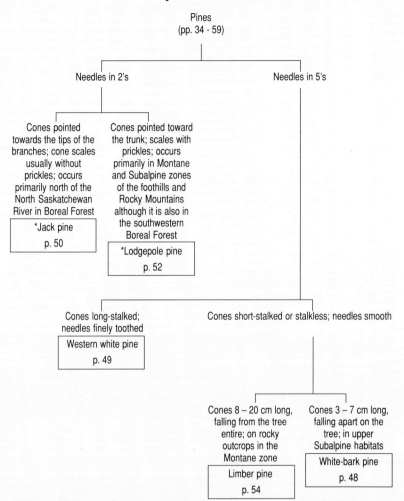

Pines
(pp. 34 - 59)

Needles in 2's

Needles in 5's

Cones pointed towards the tips of the branches; cone scales usually without prickles; occurs primarily north of the North Saskatchewan River in Boreal Forest

*Jack pine
p. 50

Cones pointed toward the trunk; scales with prickles; occurs primarily in Montane and Subalpine zones of the foothills and Rocky Mountains although it is also in the southwestern Boreal Forest

*Lodgepole pine
p. 52

Cones long-stalked; needles finely toothed

Western white pine
p. 49

Cones short-stalked or stalkless; needles smooth

Cones 8 – 20 cm long, falling from the tree entire; on rocky outcrops in the Montane zone

Limber pine
p. 54

Cones 3 – 7 cm long, falling apart on the tree; in upper Subalpine habitats

White-bark pine
p. 48

* Jack and lodgepole pine hybridize where their ranges overlap.

Illustrated Terminology

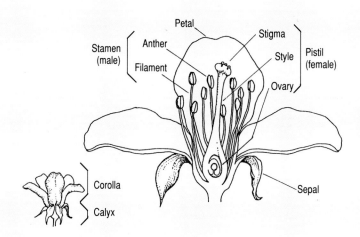

Flower parts

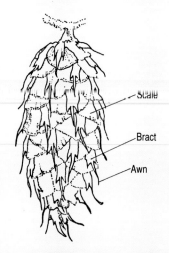

Cone parts

LEAF CHARACTERISTICS

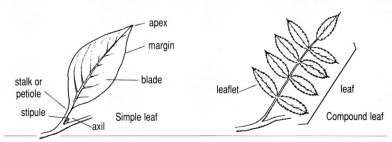

Types of leaves

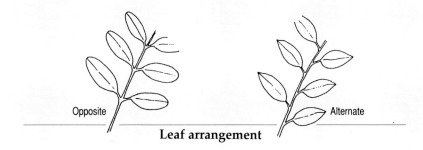

Leaf arrangement

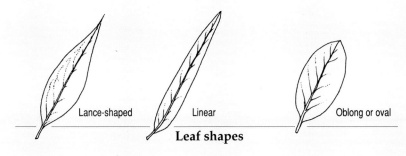

Leaf shapes

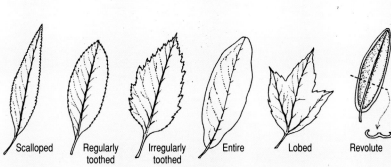

Leaf margin characteristics

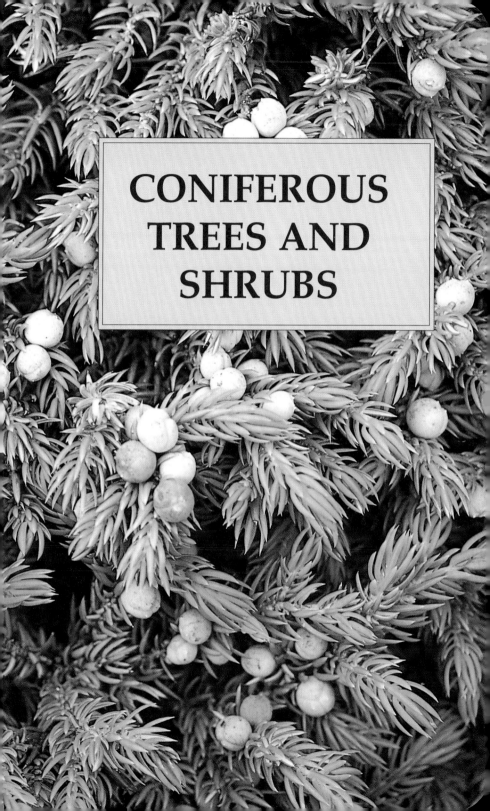

CONIFEROUS TREES AND SHRUBS

COMMON JUNIPER;
Ground Juniper
Juniperus communis
Cypress Family (Cupressaceae)

Habitat and range: Open woods and dry, rocky slopes; often on gravelly or poor soil. Widespread in the province and throughout the world.

Reproductive structures: Male and female reproductive organs in cones, usually on separate plants. Female cones appear like pale green to pale blue berries 6 – 9 mm long, containing one to three seeds. Male cones are small (3 – 5 mm long), and catkin-like.

Leaves: Forward-curved, sharp-pointed needles 5 – 15 mm long. Deeply grooved with a whitish bloom on the upper surface. Strong-smelling.

Growth habit: Evergreen, prostrate to semi-erect shrub to 1 m high, with grey or reddish-brown shredding bark. Forms large, distinctive dark green clumps on exposed hillsides and also in forest understories.

The scientific name *Juniperus* is the Latin for juniper while the species name *communis* is Latin for common. The Cree of Alberta used the inner bark as a poultice. Both the inner bark and the end shoots of the new growth can be brewed to make a weak diuretic tea. Junipers were used by B.C. Indians as fumigants, deodorizers, and cleansers, and the wood has been used in recent times to make fence posts and pencils.

The berries have been used by various North American tribes to produce a brown dye and to treat colic, snakebite, and lung and venereal diseases. They also have been used as food: ground into meal by early settlers; roasted to make coffee; used to flavour gin and sauerkraut,

The forward-curved needle-like leaves are stiff and sharp-pointed.

to make beer in France, and as a substitute for pepper in England. The berries have a strong taste, however, and should not be eaten in quantity as they may cause digestive upset and kidney irritation. They are also believed to be toxic to livestock.

There are approximately fifty species of juniper in the Northern Hemisphere, in habitats ranging from alpine to arid subtropical. Three species are native to Alberta.

The berry-like cones are used to flavour gin but can be toxic in large quantities.

CREEPING JUNIPER

Juniperus horizontalis
Cypress Family (Cupressaceae)

Habitat and range: Dry, sandy or rocky slopes and ridges; flood plains. Widespread throughout the province.

Reproductive structures: Male and female reproductive structures on separate plants (dioecious), in cones near the ends of the branches. Female cones are 5 – 8 mm long, appearing like dark blue berries with a white bloom when mature, light blue or light green when immature. Each female or seed cone usually contains two to six seeds. Male cones are small (4 – 5 mm long) and catkin-like.

Leaves: Juvenile leaves needle-like, sharp-pointed; similar to adult common juniper. Adult leaves bright green to deep blue-green, scale-like, 2 – 3 mm long, closely overlapping.

Growth habit: Evergreen, prostrate shrub which may form large clumps. Main branches may be very long with numerous branchlets to 30 cm high. Bark greyish, shredding.

Note how the immature growth of creeping juniper resembles that of common juniper.

The specific name *horizontalis* is Latin for growing horizontally and describes the flattened appearance of this shrub. The Blood Indians of Alberta used the needles in incense and stored them with clothes to repel insects, and they used the berries in necklaces. Creeping juniper has been used throughout the years for similar purposes as common juniper.

Creeping juniper differs from common juniper (*J. communis*) in that it has shorter, more appressed leaves (like a cedar) and a darker blue berry. The third native Alberta species, Rocky Mountain juniper (*J. scopulorum*) is similar to creeping juniper but usually has one or more erect, tree-like branches. Cultivars of both creeping and Rocky Mountain juniper are recommended for ornamental planting in Alberta.

B. ANDRUSEK

The mature leaves of creeping juniper are flatter and more closely overlapping than those of common juniper.

C. WERSHLER

Creeping juniper usually grows in prostrate, spreading clumps.

C. WERSHLER

Rocky Mountain juniper resembles creeping juniper but has a more upright growth habit.

31

WESTERN RED CEDAR
Thuja plicata
Cypress Family (Cupressaceae)

Habitat and range: Cool, moist, shady mountain slopes. Found in the Rocky Mountains along the B.C. border. Uncommon in Alberta.

Reproductive structures: Female cones round, 8 – 12 mm long, on curved stalks at the end of short branchlets. Cone scales sharp-pointed. Seeds with two membranous narrow wings. Male cones numerous, red, tiny (2 mm long).

Leaves: Small (3 – 5 mm long), flattened, smooth; scale-like in four overlapping rows.

Growth habit: Evergreen tree with spreading, upward curved branches. B.C. trees may grow to 70 m in height but Alberta specimens are much smaller. Older trees have thin, grey, shredding bark in narrow, vertical ridges. The trunk is usually buttressed at the base.

Thuja is from the ancient Greek *thuia* for an evergreen, aromatic, resinous tree. *Plicata* is Latin for folded, and refers to the flattened twigs with overlapping scale-like leaves. Western red cedar was used by B.C. Indian tribes for canoes, lodges, storage boxes, woodworking and even clothing. It is currently an important timber tree in B.C., where the light, decay-resistant, aromatic wood is used for shingles, posts, and exterior and interior furnishing.

There are four species of this genus in the world, but only one in Western Canada.

**Female
cone detail
of western
red cedar.**

Western red cedar has graceful, drooping
branches and distinctive greyish, shredding
bark.

Characteristic flattened leaves and numerous,
small cones.

BALSAM FIR
Abies balsamea
Pine Family (Pinaceae)

Habitat and range: Moist woods in the north-central and northeastern part of the province. Often grows with white spruce and poplar.

Reproductive structures: Female cones erect, cylindrical, 5–10 cm long. Awn-tipped bracts shorter than the scales, which fall off at maturity. Seeds winged. Male cones smaller, yellow-red or purple-tinged.

Leaves: Needles flat, 12–25 mm long, in two rows along the branchlets. Shiny green above with two silvery bands of stomata on the underside; occasionally some stomata above. Rounded or slightly notched at the tip.

Growth habit: Symmetrical tree to 18 m tall with a narrow, pyramidal crown. Bark smooth with resin blisters on younger trees, becoming thin and scaly with age. Shallow-rooted, therefore not wind firm.

The graceful form of balsam fir makes it popular as a Christmas tree.

Abies is the Latin name for fir, while *balsamea* is from the Latin *balsamum* referring to the resinous pockets in the bark. The inner bark of the trees was dried and ground into meal to be mixed with flour, or boiled with other ingredients and inhaled to speed childbirth by Ottawa, Blackfoot, and Chippewa Indians. The resin was chewed as a gum and used by natives to soothe cuts, burns, and relieve heart and chest pains. Ojibwa and Blackfoot drank a beverage made from the gummy sap in an effort to cure gonorrhea. Nowadays, balsam

The smooth, blistered bark is typical of young balsam fir.

fir is used for Christmas trees and pulp, and the yellow resin is marketed as Canada balsam which is used in microscopy.

There are forty species of fir in temperate zones of the world. Four species occur in Canada but only two of these are native to Alberta.

This bark will become more scaly with age.

SUBALPINE FIR; ALPINE FIR
Abies lasiocarpa
Pine Family (Pinaceae)

Habitat and range: On moist slopes of Subalpine forests in the Rocky Mountains. Scattered occurrence at lower altitudes in central Alberta. Usually grows with Engelmann spruce in mixed stands. Shade-tolerant.

Reproductive structures: Male and female cones bunched near the top of the tree at the tip of the previous year's branches. Male cones small (7 – 20 mm long), oval, hanging from the underside of branches. Female cones larger (6 – 10 cm), cylindrical, erect, dark purple-brown with rounded scales which are deciduous although the central axis of the cone may persist for years. Seeds light brown, 6 – 7 mm long, with prominent wings.

Leaves: Flattened, shiny bright green above with two white rows of stomata along the midvein above and below. Curved upwards with notched or blunt tips, 1.5 – 4.0 cm long.

Growth habit: Grows as a tree with a cone-like narrow crown, straight trunk and drooping lower branches, or as a prostrate shrub near tree-line, where branches may root to give dense cover. Young bark grey, smooth, with resin blisters. Young twigs hairy.

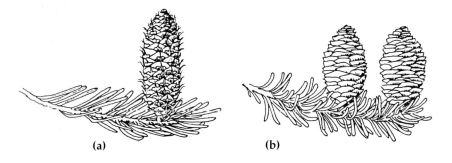

(a)   (b)

Cone and leaf detail of (a) balsam fir (b) subalpine fir. Balsam fir has flat needles in two rows while subalpine fir has upward-curving needles which are not in distinct rows.

Lasiocarpa is from the Greek *lasios* (shaggy) and *karpos* (fruit). Needles were pulverized by some Indian tribes to make baby powder, burned as incense at Blackfoot ceremonials, brewed as a tea, and used in the manufacture of medicines. Certain B.C. Indians chewed the pitch to clean their teeth and the Blackfoot used the resin as an antiseptic for wounds. The boughs were utilized by some tribes as bedding. Firs are currently popular for Christmas trees and the wood is used for pulp.

Subalpine fir may be differentiated (with difficulty) from balsam fir by its forward-pointing, upward-curved needles which have numerous white stomata on both surfaces. In areas where their ranges overlap, they hybridize. Subalpine fir may be distinguished from Engelmann spruce, with which it often grows, by its flatter needles which cannot be rolled between the fingers.

Krummholz form of subalpine fir in exposed, high altitude locations.

TAMARACK;
Hackmatack; American Larch
Larix laricina
Pine Family (Pinaceae)

Habitat and range: Common in central and northern Alberta muskegs. Commonly associated with black spruce and dwarf birch on poorly drained soils; occasionally found in pure stands. Shade-intolerant.

Reproductive structures: Female cones light brown, small (1 – 2.5 cm long), with thin, smooth scales and pointed bracts. Found on leafy branches. Seeds tiny, winged. Male cones small, round; at the end of naked shoots. Both male and female cones on the same tree. Persistent.

Leaves: Pale-green, soft needle-like leaves occur singly on elongated twigs at the ends of branches and in clusters of 15 – 25 or more on dwarf twigs. Needles somewhat three-angled, 1 – 2.5 cm long, spirally arranged on branches. Larches differ from our other conifers in that they are deciduous; in the fall the leaves turn yellow and drop off.

C. WERSHLER

Tamarack is common in boreal forest muskeg.

Growth habit: Slender, red-brown, rough-barked tree to 20 m tall. In the north it is often shorter and stunted in appearance with narrower crown and fewer leaves. Trunks straight, with little taper. The tree has an open appearance due to the straight branches (rather than drooping or ascending), and fine, short needles. Twigs slender, orange-brown, hairless.

Larix is the Latin name for larch and *laricina* is Latin for larch-like. Certain Indian tribes chewed the gum of larch species to relieve indigestion and the new shoots were said to be edible in times of emergency. When ships were made of wood, larch roots were used to join ribs to deck timbers. Wood from larch species is still used in some areas for railway ties, poles, pulp, broom handles, flooring, and the bark is a source of tannin for tanning leather.

B. ANDRUSEK

Soft, clustered needles of tamarack.

ALPINE LARCH;
LYALL'S LARCH;
Subalpine Larch
Larix lyallii
Pine Family (Pinaceae)

Habitat and range: High elevation Subalpine zones in the mountains, usually on rocky, gravelly soil. Often forms pure stands near tree-line.

Reproductive structures: Seed cones 2 – 5 cm long, with wavy scales and slender, long-awned bracts. Cone scales hairy along the margin and covered with white, tangled hairs below. Seeds winged, 3 mm long. Male cones yellow, to 1.5 cm long.

Leaves: Needle-like, 30 – 40 per cluster on dwarf twigs, occurring singly on elongated twigs. Slender, soft, 2.5 – 4 cm long. Light green, turning yellow in the autumn when they drop from the tree.

Growth habit: Small (to 15 m) tree with red-brown or grey scaly bark. Twigs stout, covered with white, tangled hairs which turn black. Mature trees very ragged-looking due to dead branches and branches of different lengths.

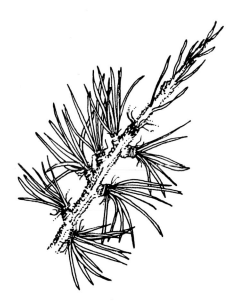

Alpine larch

Western larch

Alpine larch showing hairy twigs and two different types of leaf arrangement.

Difference in leaf shape between alpine and western larch. Alpine larch has two resin ducts, western larch has none.

The species is named after a Scottish surgeon and naturalist, David Lyall, who accompanied numerous British expeditions and surveys.

Soup can apparently be made from the young twigs as a survival food but there is little information available on other edible or medicinal uses of Lyall's larch.

There are about ten species of larch, all in the temperate and subarctic regions of the Northern Hemisphere. Three occur in Alberta. Western larch (*Larix occidentalis*) has three-angled leaves and smooth twigs as contrasted with the four-angled leaves and long-hairy twigs of alpine

The fall colour of alpine larch forms a striking contrast against upper subalpine evergreens and snow.

larch. Western larch occurs in the mountains near the B.C. border in southwestern Alberta, and is rare in the province. Tamarack, the only other native Alberta larch, has smaller seed cones than alpine or western larch (generally less than 2.5 cm) and bracts shorter than the scales. In addition, alpine larch is a species of the southwestern mountains while tamarack is found on poorly drained soils in the northern half of the province.

41

ENGELMANN SPRUCE
Picea engelmannii
Pine Family (Pinaceae)

Habitat and range: Subalpine forest in the Rocky Mountains from approximately 900 – 2200 m. Usually occurs in a mixture with other conifers but also forms pure stands. Interbreeds with white spruce where their ranges overlap. Shade-tolerant.

Reproductive structures: Seed cones pale brown, narrowly oval, 3 – 8 cm long. Seed scales tapered at both ends, not woody, and usually ragged at the edges. Seeds winged; 3 mm long. Male cones yellow, 10 – 15 mm long.

Leaves: Leaves 1.5 – 3 cm long, blue-green, four-angled and prominently ridged beneath. Needles curved with the tips flattened and blunt to short-pointed. Two white lines of stomata on the top and underside of the leaf. Aromatic when crushed.

Growth habit: Large tree (to 30 m) with narrow spire-like crown and drooping lower branches, or short shrub at alpine elevations. Bark of older trees loose, scaly, red-brown to grey. Younger branches often finely hairy.

Picea is from the Latin *pix* for pitch, while the specific name *engelmannii* honours George Engelmann, a 19th century German-born physician and botanist who was an authority on conifers. North American Indian tribes used the wood of Engelmann spruce for snowshoe frames and bows, heated the spruce gum and used it as a glue to stick skin onto bows and arrowheads onto shafts, and used the roots of the tree in basket-making. It is an important tree in the pulp and timber industry.

Pure Engelmann spruce is found only at high elevations in the mountains.

WHITE SPRUCE;
Cat Spruce
Picea glauca
Pine Family (Pinaceae)

Habitat and range: North-facing slopes, northern forests; low to middle elevations in the mountains. Shade-tolerant. Usually grows in a mixture with other conifers and poplars. Widespread throughout Alberta and Canada.

Reproductive structures: Male and female cones both found on the same tree. Female, or seed cones, 2.5–5 cm long; deciduous. Cone scales red-brown, round; closely overlapping when young, spreading with age. Seeds thin-winged. Male cones pale red, shaped like tiny eggs on the ends of the branches.

Leaves: Sharp-pointed, four-sided, spirally arranged on twigs. Usually less than 1.5 cm long. Green to blue-green, often with a white bloom; aromatic when crushed. Spruce needles can be rolled between the fingers which distinguishes them from firs, which have flat needles.

Growth habit: Usually large (to 30 m), narrow-crowned trees with spreading or drooping branches and grey or red, scaly bark. Twigs usually hairless, grey or yellow. Shallow-rooted and therefore not wind firm.

Glauca means glaucous, derived from the Greek *glaukos* (grey) referring to the bloom on the foliage. Certain tribes made cooking baskets, canoes and baby carriers out of the wood while the pliable roots were used for lacing. The Alberta Cree are said to have chewed white spruce cones to relieve sore throats.

Today spruce wood is used for lumber, plywood, paddles, piano sounding boards, food containers, and is the most important genus in the world for pulpwood production.

At higher elevations in the mountains, white spruce gives way to Engelmann spruce, which is similar in appearance but has light brown, flexible cone scales with ragged edges. Black spruce has smaller cones (less than 2.5 cm long), and is usually narrower with a dense club-like top, has hairier twigs and grows mainly in muskegs.

White spruce commonly occurs with poplar in the Boreal Forest.

The needles are sharp-pointed and may be rolled between the fingers, which distinguishes spruce from fir. Cone scales of white spruce are usually firm and rounded at the tips.

Mature bark of white spruce is usually greyish-brown and scaly.

45

BLACK SPRUCE;
Bog Spruce; Swamp Spruce
Picea mariana
Pine Family (Pinaceae)

Habitat and range: Common in muskegs, often growing in association with Labrador tea. Also on drier soils in northerly locations and in the mountains. Primarily north of the North Saskatchewan River in the Boreal Forest region.

Reproductive structures: Seed cones oval, dark brown to purple, 2–3 cm long; drooping on branches. Wavy-margined, closely appressed cone scales open to release nearly black, prominently winged seeds during winter. The seed cones are not deciduous like those of white and Engelmann spruce, and may persist on the tree for several years. Male cones are dark red and much smaller.

Leaves: Needles blue-green, thick, stiff, to 1.5 cm long. Four-sided and usually blunt at the tip.

Growth habit: Slow-growing, small tree to 10 m tall with thin, scaly, grey-brown bark. In dense stands it is straight-trunked with few branches; often with a club-shaped crown. Twigs are brown and usually hairy. Can reproduce by seed or by layering, i.e. the lower branches become covered with litter and develop roots from which they send up a new tree. Shallow-rooted, therefore not wind-firm.

Picea is from the Latin *pix*, for pitch. The specific name *mariana* is Latin for "of Maryland." Phillip Miller, an 18th century botanist who named the

Difference in form between black spruce (left) and white spruce. Note the distinctive club-shaped top on the black spruce.

species, felt Maryland epitomized North America, although black spruce does not actually occur in the state.

Tea made from the bark and leaves is said to have cured cases of scurvy in Montreal among a group of explorers led by Jacques Cartier in the 1500s, although some authorities argue that the tea used was actually made from eastern white cedar. Certain North American tribes boiled the twigs and cones in maple syrup to make a potent spruce beer, and chewed the pitch.

Powdered resin was used on wounds to speed healing, and the wood was used to make snowshoe frames and drying racks.

Black spruce is an important tree for pulp. The long fibres add strength and are particularly useful in making paper products.

There are 40 species of spruce in the world's cool temperate to subarctic regions, with five occurring in Canada, three of which are native to Alberta.

B. ANDRUSEK

B. ANDRUSEK

Black spruce often has a characteristic "club-shaped" crown (above). Dead twigs and scaly bark produce an unkempt appearance (left).

 (a)   (b)   (c)

An Engelmann spruce cone (a) has ragged scales tapered at both ends, contrasted with the more rounded scales of (b) white spruce and (c) black spruce.

WHITE-BARK PINE;
Scrub Pine
Pinus albicaulis
Pine Family (Pinaceae)

Habitat and range: Occasional on exposed slopes and rocky ridges at high Subalpine elevations (near tree-line) in the Rocky Mountains.

Reproductive structures: Cones short-stalked, oval to nearly round, 3 – 7 cm long, purple-brown with thick scales which have wide, triangular tips. Cones grow at right angles to the tree branch and disintegrate to release large, brown, wingless seeds 8 – 12 mm long.

Leaves: Needles five per bundle, 4 – 8 cm long, stiff, slightly curved. Blue-green or light green, with smooth edges, in clusters at the ends of the branches.

Growth habit: Small tree (to 10 m), or stunted, bushy shrub in exposed locations. Often sprawling with branches prostrate on the ground and wide-spreading crowns. Bark grey and smooth with horizontal markings on young trees and in narrow, brown plates on older trees. Twigs red to white, usually hairy. Slow-growing.

B. ANDRUSEK

Pinus is the Latin name for the pine tree while *albicaulis* alludes to the whitish young bark from the Latin *albus* (white) and *caulis* (stem). The seeds of white-bark pine were eaten raw, roasted, or ground into meal by interior B.C. Indians. The inner bark was used as a food source by some Montana tribes.

The lower branches are often sprawling and prostrate on the ground.

There are ninety species of pine in the northern hemisphere, of which five occur in Alberta. There are two other species in which the needles occur in bunches of five. Limber pine (*Pinus flexilis*) resembles white-bark pine in appearance but usually occurs at lower elevations and has much longer cones (8 – 20 cm long) with lighter-coloured scales. Western white pine (*Pinus monticola*) has more cylindrical, long-stalked cones (10 – 25 cm long) with thinner scales and needles with tiny, widely spaced teeth along the edges. It is rare in Alberta, having been reported only from Waterton Lakes National Park.

White-bark pine often has a bushy, compact appearance at high elevations.

C. WERSHLER

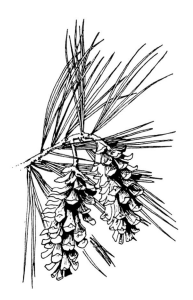

Long-stalked, cylindrical cones of western white pine.

JACK PINE
Pinus banksiana
Pine Family (Pinaceae)

Habitat and range: Sandy and gravelly areas in the Boreal Forest. In pure stands or often in mixtures with black spruce, white spruce, birch, balsam fir and poplar.

Reproductive structures: Seed cones 3–7 cm long, tan-coloured, usually curved and pointing towards the end of the branch. Scales thickened, usually smooth, occasionally with tiny prickles. Seeds black, ribbed, minute. Male cones 1 cm long, in clusters at the ends of branches.

Leaves: Yellow-green, in bundles of two, spreading, often twisted, 2–4 cm long. Sharp-pointed and usually with toothed edges. Leaf clusters have persistent, papery, basal sheaths.

Growth habit: Variable form from small and shrubby to straight, tall tree up to 20 m in height, with drooping lower branches. Older bark is red-brown and flaky, becoming deeply grooved. Twigs slender, yellow-green to dark, grey-brown.

The species name honours Sir Joseph Banks, a past president of the Royal Society of London. Jack pine was disliked by early settlers, perhaps as Hosie (1979) suggests, because it was an indicator of soils not well-suited to cultivation. The tree trunks were used by certain Alberta Indians as canoe timbers.

Today, jack pines are used in general construction and for pulp, railway ties, silos, mine timbers, and pilings.

Jack pine has flaky or grooved bark. The male cones are smaller than the female cones.

B. ANDRUSEK

Jack pine-reindeer lichen communities are common in dry, sandy areas of the Boreal Forest.

Form varies from small and shrubby to tall and spreading.

51

LODGEPOLE PINE
Pinus contorta var. *latifolia*
Pine Family (Pinaceae)

Habitat and range: Very common at lower elevations of the Subalpine zone of the Rocky Mountains; also in Cypress Hills. Occurs on a wide variety of soils in pure stands or associated with other species.

Reproductive structures: Seed cones tan-coloured, woody, 2–5 cm long, spreading or curved backward on the branch. Scales thickened, usually with small curved prickles. The seed cones remain on the tree when mature and usually remain closed until heat from a fire softens the resin holding the scales together, and causes them to open, releasing red-brown, winged seeds 4 – 5 mm long.

Leaves: In bundles of two enclosed in a papery, basal sheath. Stiff, twisted, sharp-pointed, and with more or less rough edges. Dark green to yellow-green, 3 – 6 cm long.

Growth habit: Generally a straight tree (to 30 m), often in dense, even-aged stands. Branches usually curve upward; confined to top third of the tree under crowded conditions. Bark thin, rough, with dark grey curved scales. Twigs orangish to dark brown.

Contorta, Latin for contorted or twisted, possibly refers to the gnarled branches of the coastal variety of this tree (*Pinus contorta*

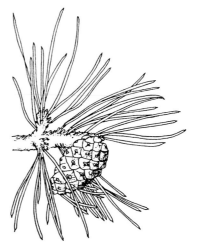

On jack pine (left) the cones are directed toward the tip of the branch while on lodgepole pine (right) the cones are directed toward the trunk of the tree.

var. *contorta*). The common name, lodgepole pine, likely denotes the use of the tree for tipi poles by the Blackfoot and Blood tribes. The wood was considered a good fuel source as it is very resinous and burns even when it is green. The resin was used to waterproof canoes, baskets, moccasins and was believed by Alberta Cree to help stop infection, soothe sore throats, and cure toothache. The inner bark is edible, particularly in the spring, and it was eaten by native peoples and settlers raw, cooked like spaghetti, or dried. It is apparently also relished by bears. The wood is now used in construction, siding and pulp.

The male cones are closely grouped and much smaller than the female cones.

Lodgepole pine closely resembles jack pine and they hybridize where their ranges overlap. However jack pine has cones directed toward the tip of the branch and scales usually without prickles at maturity. Lodgepole pine is Alberta's provincial tree.

Lodgepole pine forms dense stands after fire.

LIMBER PINE;
Rocky Mountain White Pine
Pinus flexilis
Pine Family (Pinaceae)

Habitat and range: Dry, exposed, rocky slopes and ridges in Montane and Subalpine zones in the foothills and mountains. Solitary or in small stands. Tolerates a wide variety of soils.

Reproductive structures: Seed cones short-stalked, cylindrical, large, 8–20 cm long. Light green becoming brown at maturity; scales very thick at the tip. Seeds 10–12 mm long, dark brown, often with short wings. Male cones red, much smaller, clustered at the base of the current season's shoots.

Leaves: Needles in bundles of five, clustered toward the ends of branches. Yellow-green to blue green, stiff, curved, with smooth edges, 3–8.5 cm long.

Growth habit: Small, often twisted tree (to 12 m); usually shrubby in exposed conditions. Bark smooth, light grey, becoming dark brown and scaly with age. Young branches hairy at first, green, turning grey with age. On older trees, the lower branches become very long, sometimes longer than the height of the tree. The lower branches often droop, with the tips curved upwards. Limber pine is slow-growing and long-lived.

The supple young branches give the tree its common name of limber pine. *Flexilis* is Latin for bendable and may refer to the basal cone scales of the limber pine.

Limber Pine is similar to white-bark pine, but has longer cones and usually occurs on rocky ridges at lower elevations.

Fir   Spruce   Pine

Cross-sections of fir, spruce and pine needles. Note that fir needles are flattened, spruce needles four-angled and pine needles curved.

B. ANDRUSEK

Mature cones may grow to 20 cm long.

In exposed locations, a gnarled appearance is common.

Limber pine is characteristically found on rocky ridges in the foothills.

DOUGLAS FIR;
DOUGLAS-FIR

Pseudotsuga menziesii
Pine Family (Pinaceae)

Habitat and range: A characteristic species of the Montane zone, Douglas fir occasionally ascends to tree-line in the mountains. It occurs in pure or mixed stands on moist to very dry soils. Essentially a mountain species, it occasionally extends eastward into the prairies along river valleys.

Reproductive structures: Seed cones 4 – 10 cm long, light red-brown with three-pronged bracts projecting beyond hard, rounded scales. Female cones droop from the branches; mature in one season. Seeds broadly-winged, 5 – 6 mm long. Male cones 5 – 10 mm long, often reflexed on the underside of the branches.

Leaves: Flat, 2 – 3.5 cm long, narrowed and twisted at the base. Dark green or blue-green and grooved above, paler beneath with two long bands of stomata separated by a prominent midvein.

Growth habit: The largest tree in Canada but smaller here than in British Columbia, where it can reach 70 m in height. Massive with thick, deeply grooved light to dark brown bark and spreading to drooping branches. Older trees often branch-free for much of their length. Bark of younger trees smooth with resin blisters.

This tree was named after David Douglas of the Royal Horticultural Society of England, who made many botanical explorations in North America. *Pseudotsuga* is from the Greek *pseudo*s (false) and *tsuga,*

The needles are flattened and smooth to the touch (above). The bark of mature Douglas fir is deeply grooved and has a striped appearance (left).

the Japanese name for hemlock, although the two species are quite different in appearance. The species name commemorates Archibald Menzies, the Scottish physician and naturalist, who discovered Douglas fir.

Indians used the seeds of Douglas fir for food and made tea from the young twigs and needles. The inner bark was eaten fresh or pressed into cakes by the Blackfoot, and the sap was chewed to treat colds. The heavy, strong, wood made durable tipi poles, spear shafts and snowshoes.

Today Douglas fir is an important timber tree, and is used in Alberta for such purposes as flooring, plywood, structural timber and telephone poles.

There are five species of this genus in the world (mainly in Eastern Asia and Japan) but only one in Canada.

Cone of Douglas fir showing distinctive three-pronged bracts.

Douglas fir is the largest tree in Canada.

WESTERN HEMLOCK
Tsuga heterophylla
Pine Family (Pinaceae)

Habitat and range: Moist Subalpine forest in a few locations in the mountains. Shade-tolerant and often found in dense forest. Rare in Alberta.

Reproductive structures: Seed cones green, becoming dark brown, 1.5 – 2.5 cm long, oblong, blunt-tipped when open, short-stalked, usually drooping. Scales thin, concave and rounded. Seeds winged, 4 mm long, brown, dotted with minute resin blisters. Male cones yellow, 3 – 4 mm long.

Leaves: Variable length (5 – 25 mm long), flattened, dark green or yellow-green above, white below in two bands. Rounded or indented at the tip and narrowed at the base to a thin stalk.

Growth habit: Large tree in British Columbia (to 50 m) but much smaller in Alberta. The tip of the tree (leader) usually droops, as do the branches. Outer bark dark brown to red-brown, ridged. Inner bark red or purplish. Young twigs often hairy, slender.

Early settlers named hemlock after a European weed with a similar odour. The scientific name *tsuga* is the Japanese name for the native hemlocks of Japan, while the species name *heterophylla* is Latin for leaves of different sizes or shapes, from the Greek *heteros* (different) and *phyllon* (leaf).

The slimy inner bark was eaten and used for a dye and wood preservative by certain B.C. Indians and the tannin-rich bark was used for tanning. The strong, durable wood was used for implements such as spear shafts, spoons, combs, and fish hooks. Bedding was made from the flattened boughs with their soft, flat needles. Western hemlock is very important for timber, plywood and pulp in B.C.

There are ten species of hemlock in the world, three in North America, only one of which occurs in Alberta.

C. WALLIS

The flared cones and smooth, flattened
needles of western hemlock.

K. WILKINSON

The drooping tip, or leader, is characteristic.

WESTERN YEW;
Pacific Yew
Taxus brevifolia
Yew Family (Taxaceae)

Habitat and range: Moist woodland in Waterton Lakes National Park. Rare in Alberta.

Reproductive structures: Male and female reproductive organs usually on separate plants (dioecious). Male cones 3 mm long with minute, yellow stamens in tiny, round clusters with small bracts at the bases. Seed brown or dark blue, hard, oval, 5–6 mm long, surrounded by a red fleshy cup (aril).

Leaves: Flat, needle-like, 1–2.5 cm long. Shiny, light green above, paler below. Spirally arranged, spine-tipped and tapered at the base to a short, twisted stalk.

Growth habit: Evergreen shrub at high elevations or small, often twisted tree, 5–15 m tall, with slender, drooping or spreading branches. Bark red-brown, thin, scaly. Young twigs green.

The generic name *Taxus* is from the Greek *taxos* (bow). *Brevifolia* means short-leaved from the Latin *brevis* (short) and *folium* (leaf). The flexible, strong wood was used by native peoples in the manufacture of bows but also for canoe paddles, clubs, sewing needles, fish hooks, knives, and snowshoe frames. Although the fleshy arils were eaten in small quantities by certain B.C. Indians, the seeds, bark and foliage of many yew species are highly poisonous, containing taxine, a very potent alkaloid.

Branches of yew were used in ancient times to symbolize bereavement.

There are seven species of yew in north temperate zones but only one in Alberta.

The distinctive fruits (left) and male flowers (right) of western yew.

The shiny, spine-tipped leaves and red, fleshy aril are distinctive. The leaves, seeds and bark of many yew species are highly poisonous.

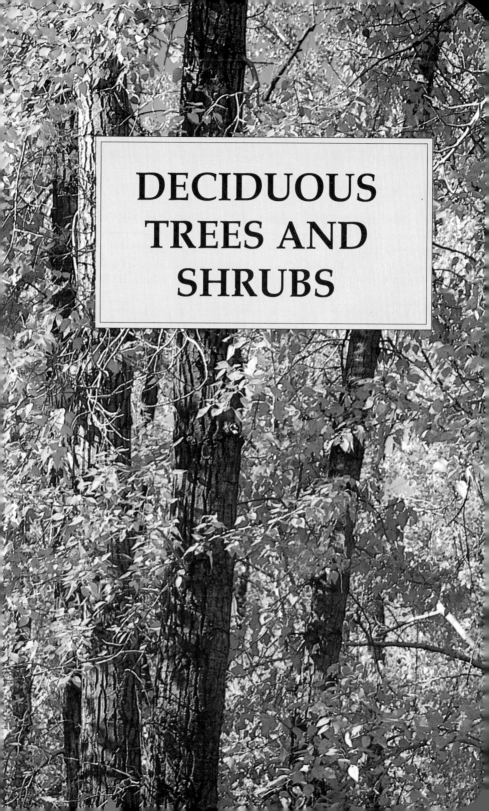

DECIDUOUS
TREES AND
SHRUBS

NARROW-LEAF COTTONWOOD
Populus angustifolia
Willow Family (Salicaceae)

Habitat and range: River valleys in southwestern Alberta from the Bow River southward. Moist soils of gravel and sand bars. Shade-intolerant.

Reproductive Structures: Male and female reproductive organs on separate plants. Male and female flowers in drooping, single-stemmed clusters, which appear before leaves; male 2 – 3 cm long, female 4 – 10 cm long.

Fruit: A narrowly oval, wrinkled capsule, 4 – 6 mm long, which splits open to release tiny brown seeds with long silky hairs.

Leaves: Alternate, simple, willow-like. Bright green above; paler below, 5 – 10 cm long, short-stalked (leaf stalks to one third as long as the blade). Lance-shaped blade gradually narrowed to the tip, scalloped along the edges, wedge-shaped to rounded at base.

Growth habit: Small (to 12 m) slender tree, with ascending branches. Bark smooth with green-white bloom on young trees; thick and grooved on older trunks. Twigs slender, yellow-brown, turning whitish. Grows rapidly but short-lived (like most poplars).

Populus is from the Latin name for the tree and the species name *angustifolia* means narrow-leaved, from the Latin *angustus* (narrow) and *folium* (leaf).

In contrast to other Alberta poplars, the leaves are narrow and gradually tapered to the tip.

B. ANDRUSEK

The inner bark (cambium) was eaten and smoked by the Blackfoot, and the wood was used for fuel and shelter. Other North American tribes dipped the cottony flower in water and placed it on infected gums or teeth. Fresh flowers were used in brews to stop internal bleeding and, in the spring, a tea of the flowers was drunk to purify the blood. The sap is edible raw or cooked, and the resinous buds and catkins, bark, twigs and leaves are eaten by grouse, rabbits, moose and beaver.

The wood of poplar species, which is soft, is currently used for veneer, boxes, pulp, excelsior and matches.

There are forty-five species of poplar worldwide and four in Alberta. They hybridize, which can make identification difficult. The narrow leaves and short leaf stalks differentiate narrow-leaf cottonwood from the other Alberta species.

Narrow-leaf cottonwood stands occur along river valleys in southern Alberta.

BALSAM POPLAR;
Tacamahac; Black Cottonwood;
Balm-of-Gilead; Black Poplar
Populus balsamifera
Willow Family (Salicaceae)

Habitat and range: Forests, banks, flood plains, moist low-lying ground. Grows in pure stands or mixtures. Can withstand periodic flooding. Widespread in the province.

Reproductive structures: Male and female catkins on separate trees, drooping from branches. Male catkins 2 – 3 cm long, with numerous stamens. The female catkins, which are 8 - 20 cm long, are responsible for the poplar fluff of spring.

Fruit: Egg-shaped, often hairy capsules, to 10 mm long.

Leaves: Bright, shiny, dark green above, paler and often resin-marked beneath. Oval, rounded or wedge-shaped at base, tapering to a sharp-pointed tip. Entire to slightly toothed, 6 – 12 cm long. Leaf stalk (petiole) round, can be rolled between thumb and forefinger. Leaf buds large, scales very resinous, aromatic.

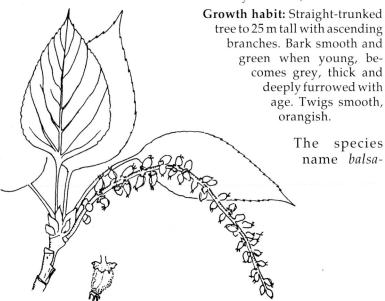

Growth habit: Straight-trunked tree to 25 m tall with ascending branches. Bark smooth and green when young, becomes grey, thick and deeply furrowed with age. Twigs smooth, orangish.

The species name *balsa-*

Female catkin of balsam poplar with an enlargement of a capsule.

mifera means balsam-bearing or with the odour of balsam, from the Latin *balsamum* (resin) and *ferre* (to bear).

The inner bark was eaten fresh or dried by the Blackfoot in emergencies and the bark has also been used to treat stomach and kidney ailments, coughs and rheumatism. The Blackfoot applied the resinous buds to the eye to cure snow blindness. The buds were used by other tribes to relieve congestion, prevent scurvy and to produce a type of glue. The buds and flowers were brewed together in a tea to purify the blood. Poplar wood was used to make dugout canoes, carved into pack-saddles and burned as fuel. Ashes from burned poplars were used as a soap substitute and the roots split and used for rope.

The balsam poplar may be distinguished from narrow-leaf cottonwood by its wider leaves and longer petioles, and from aspen poplar by its shinier, more tapered leaves and rounded, rather than flattened petioles.

Balsam poplar is common on floodplains and along creeks.

ASPEN POPLAR;
TREMBLING ASPEN;
Quaking Aspen; White Poplar
Populus tremuloides
Willow Family (Salicaceae)

Habitat and range: Widespread throughout the province and across Canada, on well-drained but moist soil. Occurs in pure stands (especially as a young tree) or mixed with other trees. Shade-intolerant.

Reproductive structures: Male catkins 2 – 3 cm long. Female catkins 4 – 10 cm long with many, slender, cone-shaped capsules 3 – 7 mm long.

Fruit: Capsules wrinkled, with two compartments which split to release the brown seeds, which are tufted with long white hairs.

Leaves: Dark, dull green above; paler below, turning bright yellow in the fall. Flattened petiole as long or longer than the leaf blade. Leaves 2 – 6 cm long, nearly round, truncate at base, abruptly sharp-pointed at the tip, usually with wavy margins or rounded teeth.

Growth habit: Slender tree to 30 m tall with few branches. Smooth, greenish to beige bark, which develops black, roughened patches and becomes furrowed with age. Twigs shiny, slender, brown to grey and buds shiny but not resinous. Reproduces mainly by suckering.

The specific name *tremuloides* is derived from the Latin *tremulus* (trembling) and the Greek *-oides* (appearing like). Because of the long flattened petioles, the leaves move with the slightest breeze, hence the name trembling or quaking aspen. In several languages, the local name for trembling aspen translates as "woman's tongue" (Hosie 1979).

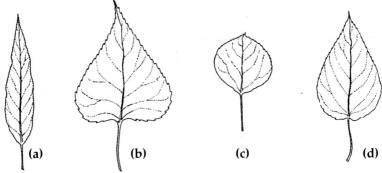

Contrasting leaf shapes of (a) narrow-leaf cottonwood, (b) western cottonwood, (c) aspen poplar, and (d) balsam poplar.

Aspen poplar may occur in pure stands or mixed with other trees.

The leaves of aspen poplar are long-petioled, and have a dull, rather than shiny surface.

Contrast between smooth, greenish bark of younger aspen poplar and roughened bark of older trees.

Aspen poplar bark contains salicin which is believed to decompose to a salicyclic acid-like compound (the main ingredient in aspirin) in humans. It has been used to treat fevers, coughs and as a diuretic, and was regarded as a famine food by the Cree and Blackfoot. The Blackfoot also used the wood for fuel, and to make dugout canoes and tent poles.

The western cottonwood (*Populus deltoides*), found in the southeastern quarter of the province, is somewhat similar to aspen poplar but has larger, more triangular leaves with more pronounced teeth along the edges.

Deeply furrowed trunk of western cottonwood.

ARCTIC WILLOW
Salix arctica
Willow Family (Salicaceae)

Habitat and range: Subalpine and Alpine open slopes and meadows near and above tree-line in the mountains.

Reproductive structures: Male and female catkins on separate plants (a characteristic of all Alberta willows and poplars), appearing at the same time as the leaves. Both male and female catkins have hairy bracts at their bases. Female catkins 2 – 6 cm long, with 25 – 50 long-hairy fruits.

Fruit: Woolly-hairy capsule, 4 – 7 mm long with dark-coloured hairy bracts at the base. Capsule splits into two to release minute seeds, tufted with white, silky hairs.

Leaves: Alternate; simple, entire. Narrowly to broadly oval, 2 – 6 cm long. Leaf tip sharply pointed to rounded; base abruptly narrowed or wedge-shaped. Young leaves with scattered white hairs; older leaves shiny and smooth above, or sparsely hairy, particularly at the margins. Lower surface paler, with a white bloom. The winter buds are covered by a single scale, a characteristic of all willows.

Growth habit: Dwarf, prostrate shrubs to 20 cm tall. Tends to form loose mats. Branches smooth to slightly hairy.

Arctic willow is common in Subalpine and Alpine meadows. Mature female catkins are illustrated here.

Salix is the Latin name for willow, related to the Celtic *sal* (near) and *lis* (water), alluding to the fact that willows are usually associated with stream banks, lake shores, etc. The species name *arctica* means arctic in Latin.

The young leaves, underground stems (rhizomes) and the inner bark were occasionally eaten by native peoples and provide important browse for ptarmigan and other alpine wildlife. As with poplars, the inner bark contains salicin which decomposes into salicyclic acid-like compounds in humans, and was used by the Blackfoot to relieve pain and fevers.

There are approximately three hundred species of willow, mostly of the Northern Hemisphere; thirty-five in Alberta. Willows are notoriously difficult to differentiate as diagnostic features (usually the catkins) are not always present, vegetative characteristics are highly variable, and many species hybridize. Therefore only four of the more common species are treated in this book.

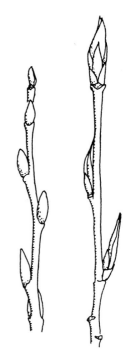

Willows (left) have one bud scale covering winter buds while poplars (right) have more than one.

BEAKED WILLOW; BEBB WILLOW
Salix bebbiana
Willow Family (Salicaceae)

Habitat and range: In wooded areas; forming thickets on flood plains, stream banks, and slough margins; occasionally on sand dunes. Widespread in the province. Beaked willow extends from Vancouver Island to Newfoundland and is the most common tree-sized willow in Canada.

Reproductive structures: Catkins appear before or with the leaves, on short branchlets. Bracts at the bases of the catkins narrowly oblong, yellow, tinged with red. Male catkins pussy willow-like, 1 – 2 cm long. Female catkins 2 – 6 cm long, composed of many beaked capsules.

Fruit: Capsules long-beaked, soft-hairy, 5 – 9 mm long. Seeds dark, tiny, with long tufts of white hairs.

Leaves: Alternate, simple, oval shaped, 2 – 6 cm long. Wider-leaved than most of our willows. Tip blunt or sharp-pointed, base round to acute, edges entire or with rounded teeth. Upper surface grey-green, paler beneath and often soft-hairy, especially along mid-rib and veins. Glaucous (with a white bloom) and sometimes deeply veined below.

Growth habit: Much-branched shrub or small tree to 5 m tall. Branches red-brown, sometimes hairy. Twigs yellowish, usually densely hairy. Older bark grey-brown, scaly.

Bebbiana honours Michael Bebb, an 19th century authority on willows. Native peoples used the slender, flexible wood to make hide-stretchers and fish traps, the twigs to clean teeth, and the bark in basket making. Willows serve an important function in reclamation of disturbed sites because they can be propagated easily by cuttings, and grow rapidly.

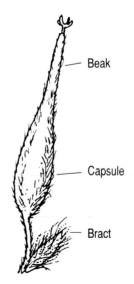

Beak

Capsule

Bract

Detail of beaked willow capsule.

The female catkins of beaked willow may be up to 6 cm long and are composed of many, beaked capsules.

Yellow willow (*Salix lutea*) often forms thickets on river banks.

Smooth willow (*Salix glauca*) is common on floodplains.

PUSSY WILLOW
Salix discolor
Willow Family (Salicaceae)

Habitat and range: Stream banks, slough margins; aspen and mixed woods. Widespread in the province and in Canada.

Reproductive Structures: Catkins usually attached directly to twigs, appearing before the leaves. Bracts dark brown to black, long-hairy. Male catkins (the familiar furry pussy willow) are 2 – 3 cm long. Female catkins 4 – 7 cm long.

Fruit: Capsules long-beaked; finely hairy, 8 – 10 mm long.

Leaves: Oval, rounded to acute at the tip and wedge-shaped at the base, 3 – 10 cm long. Margins entire and wavy or with widely spaced teeth. Young leaves silky-hairy with white or rusty-red hairs, becoming smooth with age. Upper leaf dull to shiny light green, lower silvery with a white bloom. Midvein prominent, yellow.

Growth habit: Shrub or small tree, to 10 m tall, with open, rounded crown. Branches dark brown to yellowish; twigs smooth to sparsely hairy. Mature bark greyish, grooved near the base of the shrub.

The catkins of pussy willow are popular in floral displays.

B. ANDRUSEK

The species name *discolor* is from the Latin meaning two or more colours and refers to the pussy willow leaves.

The Blackfoot made a brew of the twigs steeped in boiling water to relieve pain and fever. They also used the wood for furniture, tipi pegs and sweat-lodges, the spring buds for a red dye and the tannin in the bark to tan hides.

A wide-spreading, much-branched form is characteristic of pussy willow.

SANDBAR WILLOW; COYOTE WILLOW; SILVER WILLOW
Salix exigua
Willow Family (Salicaceae)

Habitat and range: Gravelly or sandy flood plains, banks, slough margins, in Prairies, foothills, Aspen Parkland and Boreal Forest.

Reproductive structures: Catkins occur on leafy twigs. Male catkins 3 – 4 cm long; female 1 – 7 cm long. The first catkins appear with the leaves; others appear throughout the season.

Fruit: Capsules 4 – 8 mm long, usually smooth with yellowish hairy bracts.

Leaves: Smooth, fairly thick, yellowish-green and shiny above, glaucous and lighter beneath. Leaves narrowly linear, with sharp-pointed tips and wedge-shaped bases. Margins with small distinct teeth or entire. Younger leaves somewhat hairy. Stipules to 7 mm long, deciduous.

Growth habit: Spreading shrub or small tree to 3 m tall. Often forms dense clumps from underground stems. Branches are shiny, reddish or yellowish-brown and often soft-hairy when young, turning grey or greyish-red when mature. The long, slender stems and branches and narrow leaves give this shrub a graceful appearance.

Sandbar willow is common on riverbanks. Note the long, narrow leaves.

Willows were highly regarded by native peoples of Alberta because the flexibility of the branches and bark made them useful for fish nets, rope and woven bags, mats, saddle blankets, etc. The inner bark was shredded to make diaper linings and wound dressings. Willow leaves were utilized for wrapping and serving fish, and were occasionally eaten in emergencies. Willow roots were mixed with grease from animal kidneys to treat scalp sores and dandruff.

In contrast to other willows, catkins are present for much of the growing season.

SWEET GALE;
Bog Myrtle
Myrica gale
Bayberry Family (Myricaceae)

Habitat and range: Swamps, stream banks, and thickets; mainly in extreme north-eastern Alberta in the Boreal Forest.

Reproductive structures: Male and female catkins on separate plants, appearing before the leaves. Male catkins cylindrical, crowded, 1–2 cm long with large brown bracts. Female catkins oval, cone-like, 8–10 mm long. Catkins ooze a scented yellow wax.

Fruit: Beaked nutlet 2–3 mm long with waxy glands; winged at base.

Leaves: Alternate, simple, deciduous. Lance-shaped, firm, entire or coarsely toothed toward the rounded tip, wedge-shaped at the base. Smooth or hairy, with tiny bright yellow, waxy glands on both surfaces.

Growth habit: Low shrub to 1.5 m tall, with ascending branches. New growth finely hairy, becoming smooth. Aromatic.

The generic name is from the ancient Greek *myrike* (perfume) which referred to another species of fragrant shrub. The specific name may be derived from the Latin *galea* (helmet) which possibly refers to the brown enclosing bracts of the catkins. The dried leaves may be used to make tea and both the leaves and nutlets have been used as a seasoning. The Alberta Cree are said to have used the buds as a dye for porcupine quills.

There are forty species of this genus in the Northern Hemisphere; only one in Alberta. The related bayberry, which occurs in the Pacific Northwest, is known for the "berries" (actually wax-covered seeds) which are used to make fragrant bayberry candles.

Female catkins of sweet gale. Male and female catkins are borne on separate plants.

GREEN ALDER
Alnus crispa
Birch Family (Betulaceae)

Habitat and range: Open woods, stream banks, edges of wetlands, lowland areas of sand hills. Widespread throughout the province except in the southeast quarter.

Reproductive structures: Male and female flowers in catkins on the same plant, appearing at the same time as the leaves. Male catkins in drooping clusters to 10 cm long. Female catkins cone-like, oval, with thick woody bracts, 3 – 6 per branch, 1 – 2 cm long.

Fruit: Nutlet, 2 – 3 mm long with membranous wings.

Leaves: Simple, alternate. Shining, smooth above; paler and sometimes hairy below, particularly along the veins. Broadly oval, rounded to wedge-shaped at base with a sharp-pointed tip, irregularly toothed along the margin, 2 – 8 cm long.

Growth habit: Bushy, pleasant-smelling shrubs to 3 m tall. Young bark smooth, lustrous brown with pores (lenticels) like birch. Older bark grey. Twigs hairy and slightly resinous when young. Pith three-angled.

Alnus is the Latin name for the plant, while *crispa* is Latin for curled, and refers to the leaf's appearance. Alder bark was used to smoke fish and meats because it is low in pitch and therefore does not give an unpleasant flavour. Boiled with vinegar, the bark produced a concoction used as a lice remedy. Alder bark and wood were used by the Blackfoot for carving, fuel, and to produce a dye. The Cree used alder wood to make utensils. Pipe-stems have been made from the smaller branches.

Broad-winged nutlet of green alder (above) compared to nutlet of river alder (below).

Alders have nitrogen-fixing bacteria in nodules on their roots which convert nitrogen into nutrients for the plant. Thus when the alder dies, nitrogen is added to the soil.

There are thirty species of alder, mainly in the Northern Hemisphere; two in Alberta. River alder (*Alnus tenuifolia*) differs from green alder in that it is usually taller and is often a tree rather than shrub. River alder has much less pronounced wings on the nutlet, and flowers that develop before the leaves, which are dull, rather than shiny.

Green alder is widespread in moist areas throughout the province.

Male catkins above; the previous year's female catkins below.

In contrast to green alder, river alder has dull, rather than shiny, leaves.

BOG BIRCH; DWARF BIRCH; Ground Birch

Betula glandulosa
Birch Family (Betulaceae)

Habitat and range: Muskegs, marshes, stream banks and lake shores, open Subalpine forests and slopes. Shade-intolerant.

Reproductive structures: Male and female catkins on the same plant. Male catkins with flowers in a dense drooping cluster, to 2 cm long. Female catkins erect, 1–2 cm long, with three-lobed, finely hairy, reddish bracts.

Fruit: The fruit, called a samara, is a single-seeded, flat nutlet, 2–3 mm long, with narrow, membranous wings. The surrounding bracts disintegrate when ripe, in contrast to alders, which have persistent bracts.

Leaves: Simple, alternate, deciduous. Shiny bright green, somewhat leathery, 1–2 cm long. Paler beneath, often with tiny glands. Rounded at tip and rounded to wedge-shaped at base, 1–2 cm long, with three or fewer prominent lateral veins and ten or fewer teeth per side.

Growth habit: Erect or low and spreading shrub to 2 m tall, with grey to black stems and glandular twigs. Similarly to other Alberta birches, the bark is marked with horizontal openings (lenticels), but the bark of the bog birch does not peel readily.

Leaf and flower detail of bog birch.

The name *Betula* is probably from the Celtic *betú* meaning tree while the species name *glandulosa* means bearing glands. Bog birch is a source of food for grouse, songbirds, moose, elk and deer.

There are approximately forty species of birch in the north temperate regions and five in Alberta. The only other small, shrubby birch, dwarf birch (*B. pumila*), has hairier twigs, four or more lateral veins, ten or more teeth on the leaves and wider wings on the samaras (they are lumped together as variants of a single species by some taxonomists).

As with alders, there is some disagreement over species taxonomy and the species hybridize to add to the confusion. Birches may be distinguished from alders in that the fruiting catkins disintegrate when mature; in alders they are persistent as small woody "cones."

The round, leathery leaves and small female catkin of bog birch.

Bog birch is common in moist habitats in Boreal Forests and to Subalpine elevations in the mountains.

WHITE BIRCH; PAPER BIRCH;
Canoe Birch
Betula papyrifera
Birch Family (Betulaceae)

Habitat and range: Along streams and lakes in Boreal Forest, lower Montane slopes and Aspen Parkland. Prefers well-drained sandy or silty soil. Shade-intolerant, therefore often found in burned or cleared areas. Widely distributed but not in the extreme southeast of the province.

Reproductive structures: Male catkins in drooping, cylindrical clusters, up to 10 cm long. Female catkins paired or single on spur shoots, erect, 3 – 5 cm long, with three-lobed finely hairy bracts, 5 – 7 mm long.

Fruit: Rounded, wide-winged nutlets, 4 mm wide; three per bract.

Leaves: Simple, alternate, conspicuously veined. Dull, dark green above, paler beneath; turning yellow in the fall. Oval to nearly round, with rounded base and sharp-pointed tip, toothed (often doubly) 4 – 8 cm long.

Growth habit: A slender, long-branched tree to 30 m tall. Mature bark attractive, white or reddish-brown, marked with darker lenticels and usually peeling off in strips. Young twigs reddish with raised glands.

Papyrifera is Latin for paper-bearing, from the Greek *papyros* (paper reed) and the Latin *ferre* (to bear). The Cree used the bark and wood for canoes, baskets, bowls, and ground it in a mixture with other ingredients as a dusting powder; the Blackfoot used it to make snowshoes and sleighs.

The inner bark is said to be edible, raw or cooked. Oil in the bark contains methyl salicylate and a poultice of the boiled bark was used to treat bruises, wounds and burns. The Cree are said to have brewed the leaves into a type of tea and used the sap for a syrup. Birch wood is currently used for veneers, cabinets and woodenware.

The Alaska birch (*B. neoalaskana*) may be differentiated from other Alberta birch trees by its usually densely glandular twigs and shiny, more triangular-shaped leaves. It is found in the northern half of the province in muskegs and sand hills. Water birch (*B. occidentalis*) has a shrubbier form, with darker, shiny, non-peeling bark and smaller, often shiny leaves. It is found primarily in the southern half of the province while paper birch is more northerly. Both water birch and paper birch are grown as ornamentals in Alberta.

The characteristic white, peeling bark of white birch.

Water birch has a shrubbier form than white birch and darker bark which does not peel.

Alaska birch has shinier, more triangular-shaped leaves than white birch.

BEAKED HAZELNUT; WILD FILBERT

Corylus cornuta
Birch Family (Betulaceae)

Habitat and range: Dry thickets and woods in the north-central part of the province.

Reproductive structures: Male and female catkins on the same shrub (monoecious). Male catkins yellowish, slender, drooping, 4–7 cm long at the ends of the previous season's branches. Female flowers few, inconspicuous in short catkins concealed by bracts near the end of short branches, with only the dark red stigmas showing.

Fruit: Hard-shelled filbert-like nut, to 1.5 cm long, surrounded by green tube-like bracts. Bracts densely bristly-hairy at the base and sharply lobed at the top. Often in pairs with bases attached at the ends of the twigs.

Leaves: Simple, alternate. Broadly oval, sharp-pointed at the tip; toothed along the margin, and rounded to heart-shaped at the base, 4–10 cm long. Paler beneath and slightly hairy, especially along the veins.

Growth habit: Bushy, spreading shrub to 3 m tall with grey-brown bark. Twigs hairy when young (often with glands), becoming smoother with age.

The lobed bracts, which form a sheath around the nuts, account for the common name beaked hazelnut. The generic name is from *korys* (helmet) and the specific name *cornuta* means horned, another reference to the enclosing bracts.

The nuts are edible, once the persistent sheaths and shells are removed, and can be roasted or ground into flour. They are relished by jays, nutcrackers, crows, bears and squirrels, and the dense branches of the hazelnut provide cover and nesting sites for birds. The young, straight sucker shoots were used by some Indian tribes to make arrows, and peeled to make ropes. The roots and inner bark steeped in water produced a blue dye. Beaked hazelnuts are grown occasionally as ornamentals in Alberta.

There are approximately twelve species of hazelnut, primarily in the world's north temperate zones; one species in Alberta.

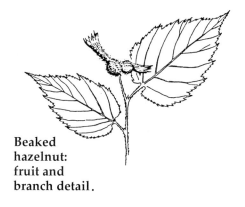

Beaked
hazelnut:
fruit and
branch detail.

C. WERSHLER

Drooping male catkins.

B. ANDRUSEK

Beaked hazelnut is found in dry areas
in the north-central part of the
province.

B. ANDRUSEK

The fruits are paired
and surrounded by
bristly, lobed bracts.

87

NUTTALL'S ATRIPLEX;
SALT SAGE;
Moundscale

Atriplex nuttallii
Goosefoot Family (Chenopodiaceae)

Habitat and range: Saline badlands, eroded slopes, exposed areas, and flood plains. Primarily from the North Saskatchewan River southward, although also present in the Peace River country.

Flowers: Male and female flowers lacking petals, inconspicuous, on separate plants. Male flowers in dense, yellow, leafy clusters at the tops of the plants (terminal). Female flowers in round heads in short, leafy clusters and in terminal leafless, closely packed groups. Blooms July-August.

Fruit: Round, hard and inflated, this spiny fruit (utricle) contains one seed, 2 mm long. Surrounded by tiny, spongy, toothed bracts.

Leaves: Numerous, simple, alternate. Linear to lance-shaped with smooth margins (entire), gradually narrowed to the bases. Grey; fine-mealy, 1 – 5 cm long. Lower stem leaves usually have clusters of small leaves in the axils.

Growth habit: Erect or spreading much-branched shrub, 20 – 60 cm tall from a woody base. Densely silvery-mealy throughout. Deep-rooted.

The generic name is from the Latin name for the plant and the specific name honours Thomas Nuttall, an English-born botanist who made many trips across the U.S.A. collecting plants, and later became the curator of the Harvard Botanical Garden.

The leaves and young stems of Nuttall's atriplex are edible raw or cooked, although they are quite salty. The seeds of some species were ground into meal, and a pulp made from chewing the stems was placed on insect bites by certain American Indian tribes.

There are over one hundred species of *Atriplex* worldwide, mainly in semi-arid to desert areas on saline or alkaline soil. Two shrubby and ten herbaceous species of *Atriplex* occur in Alberta. Shadscale (*A. canescens*), the other shrubby species, found rarely in Alberta on saline flats in the southern half of the province, may be differentiated from Nuttall's atriplex because it is woody throughout (not just at the base) and taller. Both species are mildly poisonous to livestock as they absorb selenium from the soil.

K. WILKINSON

Nuttall's atriplex is common on mudflats and eroded slopes.

Distinctive hard,
inflated fruit of
Nuttall's atriplex.

GREASEWOOD

Sarcobatus vermiculatus
Goosefoot Family (Chenopodiaceae)

Habitat and range: Saline or alkaline soils on exposed hillsides and around sloughs in the southeastern Prairies.

Flowers: Male and female flowers small, inconspicuous, monoecious, lacking petals. Male flowers small, aggregated into cone-like spikes at the ends of the branches. Female flowers solitary in leaf axils.

Fruit: Achene (dry, one-seeded fruit which remains closed at maturity) 4 – 5 mm long, surrounded by a broad, papery wing.

Leaves: Fleshy, narrow, pale yellow-green, 1 – 4 cm long.

Growth habit: Erect, much-branched shrub to 2.5 m tall (usually shorter in Alberta). Younger branches yellowish white, smooth or white-hairy. Lower branches often transformed into thorns, upper branches lacking thorns.

Sarcobatus is from the Greek *sarkos* (flesh) and *batos* (bramble) which describes the plant's fleshy leaves and spiny branches. The specific name *vermiculatus* is from the Latin for worm-like and refers to the leaf shape. Greasewood is poisonous to livestock if eaten in large quantities, as it contains sodium and potassium oxalates. It can also cause skin rashes in humans.

There are one or two species of greasewood in dry western North America; one in Alberta.

Fruit of greasewood showing papery wing.

Male flowers, leaves and branches of greasewood.

Greasewood occurs on dry hillsides and around sloughs in the southeastern prairies.

The lower branches are often thorny, the upper lack thorns.

CREEPING MAHONIA;
OREGON-GRAPE;
Rocky Mountain Grape;
Mountain Holly

Berberis repens
Barberry Family (Berberidaceae)

Habitat and range: Montane to Subalpine dry, open slopes and open aspen or spruce-fir woods in southwestern Alberta.

Flowers: Six bright yellow, oblong petals to 6 mm long, in two series. Six sepals and stamens. Fragrant. Blooms May-June.

Fruit: Grape-like blue berries up to 14 mm long, with a white bloom. Berries juicy but sour, containing a few large seeds.

Leaves: Alternate, persistent over winter. Pinnately compound with three to seven leathery leaflets, 3–8 cm long. Shiny or dull green above, paler underneath; turning to red or purple-tinged in the fall. Leaf margins with spines, similar to the familiar holly.

Growth habit: Low, erect or trailing leafy shrub, 10–30 cm tall. Bark light green or grey.

The common name Mahonia honours Bernard McMahon, an early American botanist. The generic name is from the Arabic *berberys* for a related plant and the specific name *repens* means creeping.

Alberta Blood Indians ate the berries, brewed them into a potion to relieve sore kidneys, and crushed them to treat sores and boils. The berries can be used to make juice or jelly but caution is advised as members of the barberry family contain the alkaloid drug berberine, which is toxic in large quantities. The inner bark and roots have been used for dyes, tonics, and blood purifiers by tribes such as the Blackfoot.

There are approximately three hundred species of *Berberis*, mostly in Asia and South America; only one in Alberta. Tall mahonia (*B. aquifolium*) which is closely related and similar in appearance to creeping mahonia, is the state flower of Oregon.

The berries look like grapes but should be eaten with caution.

The showy yellow flowers occur in dense clusters.

MOCK-ORANGE; SYRINGA
Philadelphus lewisii
Hydrangea Family (Hydrangeaceae)

Habitat and range: Moist, Montane woods, gullies, rocky hillsides, stream banks. In Waterton Lakes National Park and also reported at the western boundary of Alberta on the Oldman River.

Flowers: Showy, fragrant. In dense clusters at the ends of short, lateral branches. Petals four or five, white, oblong, rounded or notched at the tip, 1 – 2 cm long. Sepals four or five, broad but sharp-pointed, pale green, sparsely white-hairy at the tip, 7 mm long. Stamens unequal, 20 – 40, with bright yellow tips. Flowers in July.

Fruit: Dark brown, woody four-valved capsule, pointed at both ends. Contains many tiny seeds, 3 mm long.

Leaves: Simple, opposite. Pale green, oval to lance-shaped, 2 – 7 cm long, with a pointed tip. Margins entire or with spine-like teeth. Prominently veined, smooth or stiff-hairy. Short petioled.

Growth habit: Much-branched erect or spreading shrub 1 – 2.5 m tall. Young twigs smooth, dark red. Mature bark light brown, shredding.

The flowers are similar in appearance and fragrance to orange blossoms, hence the common name mock-orange. Syringa is actually the scientific name for lilacs, from the Greek *syrinx* (trumpet). *Philadelphus* is from the Greek *philos* (love) and *adelphos* (brother) and is said to commemorate Pharaoh Ptolemy II Philadelphus, the late Egyptian king. The specific name honours Captain Meriwether Lewis of the famous Lewis and Clark expedition.

The wood of mock-orange is strong and hard and was used to make implements such as spear shafts, bows and arrows, clubs, pipe stems, combs and blowguns by the B.C. interior tribes. The leaves lather when bruised, and were rubbed in the hands to make soap. Cultivated varieties of mock-orange are planted as ornamentals in Alberta.

The are fifty species of mock-orange in the tropical and temperate zones of North America and Asia; only one in Alberta.

C. WERSHLER

Native mock-orange is rare in Alberta, confined to Waterton Lakes National Park and vicinity.

C. WERSHLER

The flowers provide a showy, fragrant display.

Fruit and leaf arrangement of mock-orange.

GOLDEN CURRANT;
Squaw Currant
Ribes aureum
Currant and Gooseberry Family
(Grossulariaceae)

Habitat and range: River banks, rocky slopes, flood plains in the southeastern part of the province.

Flowers: Showy. Fragrant tube-like flowers to 1 cm long in ascending or reflexed clusters. Petals five, attached to the top of the tube, yellow, often with orange tips. Sepals five, yellow, spreading, 5 – 7 mm long. Blooms May – June.

Fruit: Black, red or occasionally yellow edible berry, to 8 mm long.

Leaves: Thick, pale yellow-green, 2 – 5 cm broad. Oval, deeply three-lobed and often toothed at the tips of the lobes. Wedge-shaped at the base. Leaf stalk (petiole) about as long as the blade.

Growth habit: Erect or rounded much-branched shrub, 1 – 3 m tall. Branches reddish when young, smooth to finely-hairy. Becoming smooth and dark grey with age.

The generic name *Ribes* is thought to be from the old Danish colloquial *ribs* for red currant or from *ribas*, the Arabic name for an unrelated rhubarb-like plant. *Aureum* means golden and refers to the abundant yellow flowers. Golden currant is a popular ornamental shrub because of its attractive flowers and edible fruit. The fruit was occasionally eaten raw by Indian tribes although it has a strong flavour. Today it is frequently used in jams, jellies and syrups.

There are more than a hundred species of currants and gooseberries, mostly of temperate and colder regions of the Northern Hemisphere. Eleven of these are found in Alberta, although only five are discussed in this book. *Ribes* species with prickles and spines are usually classed as gooseberries while those lacking this protection are referred to as currants.

The berries of golden currant may be reddish, yellowish or black.

C. WALLIS

In contrast to other Alberta currants, the flowers are large and showy.

B. ANDRUSEK

WILD BLACK CURRANT; NORTHERN BLACK CURRANT

Ribes hudsonianum
Currant and Gooseberry Family
(Grossulariaceae)

Habitat and range: Widespread throughout the province in moist, shaded woods and along stream banks. Forms thickets at the edge of mountain meadows.

Flowers: Erect or ascending clusters of 6 – 12 flowers. Petals five, oblong, white, 1.5 – 2.0 mm long, surrounded by five white, hairy sepals, to 4 mm long. Bases of flowers often dotted with resinous glands.

Fruit: Black berry 7 – 12 mm long, often covered with a white bloom. Bitter-tasting.

Leaves: Simple, alternate, 3 – 10 cm broad. Shaped somewhat like a maple leaf with three to five broad lobes. Heart-shaped at base, margins slightly toothed. Hairy, especially below, and with yellow, resinous glands beneath.

Growth habit: Erect or ascending low shrub without spines or prickles, to 2 m tall. Sparsely glandular throughout with round, yellow, shining glands. Has a characteristic sweet odour.

Currants mixed with meat, other fruits and pemmican were a common food of Indian people. The Thompson Indians of B.C. believed that the presence of wild black currant around a lake indicated good fishing. Alberta Cree believed that drinking a tea made from wild black currant and skunk currant helped a woman to conceive. Currants are favoured by bears, grouse, and song-birds.

B. ANDRUSEK

Although the berries appear juicy,
they are bitter-tasting.

D. JOHNSON

The leaf is broad, and somewhat
maple leaf- shaped.

BRISTLY BLACK CURRANT; SWAMP GOOSEBERRY

Ribes lacustre
Currant and Gooseberry Family
(Grossulariaceae)

Habitat and range: Moist, open woods, stream banks, Subalpine ridges and dry, forest slopes. Mainly in the mountains and the northern half of the province.

Flowers: Inconspicuous, in seven to fifteen flowered, drooping clusters. Petals rounded, usually pink or red, flattened, 1 mm long. Sepals pale green or brown, 2 – 3 mm long. Flower stalks and bases glandular-hairy with dark purple-red hairs.

Fruit: Dark purple or black berries in clusters of three or four, 6 – 8 mm long. Covered with bristly glands.

Leaves: Deeply three- to five-lobed, lobes toothed and deeply indented; base heart-shaped or truncate, 2 – 5 cm long. Similar to a small maple leaf. Smooth to sparsely hairy along the veins.

Growth habit: Erect or ascending shrub to 1.5 m tall. Young stems finely hairy, with slender prickles and long (to 10 mm) thick spines at the nodes. Older bark smooth, grey.

The berries are edible and were eaten fresh or cooked by various Indian tribes. They have also been combined with the branches and inner bark and made into a tea to cure colds and diarrhoea. The spines, however, can cause an allergic reaction if touched by susceptible individuals.

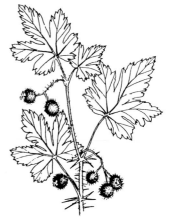

Three species of currant or gooseberry are rare in Alberta: the trailing black currant (*Ribes laxiflorum*); the mountain gooseberry (*Ribes inerme*); and sticky currant (*Ribes viscosissimum*). All three are found in Montane to Subalpine woods in the Crowsnest Pass/Waterton Lakes National Park area. Trailing black currant is also found in more northerly mountainous areas.

Bristly berries and prickly, spiny branches of black currant.

Touching the spines of this shrub can cause an allergic reaction.

Leaves and flowers.

WILD GOOSEBERRY; NORTHERN GOOSEBERRY; SMOOTH GOOSEBERRY

Ribes oxyacanthoides
Currant and Gooseberry Family
(Grossulariaceae)

Habitat and range: Moist woods along prairie streams; at low elevations in the mountains, and in the Boreal Forest. Common throughout the province.

Flowers: Inconspicuous green or white flowers in small clusters. Petals five, oblong, 2 – 2.5 mm long, with ragged tips. Sepals five, oblong, reflexed, 4 – 5 mm long. Blooms May – June.

Fruit: Yellow-green with pale green lines, maturing to a smooth, red-purple berry, 4 – 10 mm long. Edible.

Leaves: Simple, alternate, 1 – 4 cm broad. Three to five lobed, rounded to heart-shaped at base, margins with prominent unequal teeth. Usually somewhat hairy, often with glands underneath and on the petioles.

Growth habit: Erect or prostrate shrub, 1 – 2 m tall, usually with bristly stems (especially when young) and one to three spines, 1 cm long, at each node. Branches stout, yellow-brown or grey.

The berries are yellowish-green with pale green lines when immature, but purplish-black when mature.

The specific name is from the Greek *oxys* (sharp or pointed) and *akanthos* (thorn). Gooseberries were eaten fresh or dried by North American Indian tribes. The young leaves of some species were boiled and eaten with uncooked animal fat, and the thorns were used for removing splinters, and tattooing. Gooseberries are very popular for jams and jellies, especially in Britain and Europe.

The leaves may turn bright orange or red in the fall.

WILD RED CURRANT; SWAMP RED CURRANT; NORTHERN RED CURRANT

Ribes triste
Currant or Gooseberry Family
(Grossulariaceae)

Habitat and range: Moist woods and low marshy ground in Aspen Parkland and Boreal Forest. Mainly in the northern two thirds of the province.

Flowers: Six to thirteen flowers in short (to 10 cm long) drooping clusters. Clusters with small, short-stalked glands on the central axis and flower stems (pedicels). Petals five, red-purple, wedge-shaped, blunt or notched at the tips, 1 mm long. Sepals five, green-purple, 2 mm long.

Fruit: Smooth, sour-tasting red berry less than 1 cm long.

Leaves: Simple, alternate, to 12 cm broad. Broadly maple leaf-shaped, usually three-lobed (occasionally five-lobed) less than half their length. Shallowly heart-shaped or truncate at the base, coarsely toothed. Smooth above, slightly hairy and paler beneath.

Growth habit: Ascending or sprawling many-stemmed shrub, to 1 m tall, often with rooting branches. Without spines or bristles. Young twigs smooth or sparsely hairy and somewhat glandular. Older branches yellow, becoming purple-brown, shreddy.

Triste (French) means sad or dull-coloured and likely refers to the drab older branches. As with other gooseberries and currants, the fruit may be made into jelly or pies.

D. JOHNSON

The flowers occur in drooping clusters.

SASKATOON; SERVICEBERRY; Juneberry
Amelanchier alnifolia
Rose Family (Rosaceae)

Habitat and range: Common throughout the province in open woods, coulees, Prairie ravines, hillsides, Aspen Parkland; to Subalpine elevations in the mountains.

Flowers: In erect clusters at the ends of branches. Petals five, white, oblong or rounded, 5 – 20 mm long. Stamens 12 – 20, yellow. Fragrant. Blooms May – June.

Fruit: Red-purple to dark purple, glaucous berry-like pome (fruit with a central core, like an apple), 5 – 10 mm in diameter. Although they contain many seeds, the berries are sweet and juicy in years of adequate moisture.

Leaves: Simple, alternate, 2 – 5 cm long. Dark green, turning to orange or red in the fall. Oval-shaped, rounded or truncate at the tip, rounded at the base. Toothed at the tip and partway along the margins. Slightly hairy underneath becoming smooth at maturity.

Growth habit: Low, spreading shrubs or small, erect tree to 5 m tall; often in thickets. Much-branched, particularly toward the top. Branches smooth, red to brown when young, grey when older.

The Cree called this plant *mis-ask-quah-toomina* which early white settlers shortened to saskatoon. The plant is occasionally called serviceberry, due to its slight resemblance to the mountain ash or serviceberry. The generic name *Amelanchier* is said to be derived from the French name for a European species, while the specific name means alder-like foliage from the Latin *alnus* (alder) and *folium* (leaf).

The berries, which are high in iron and copper, were used fresh or dried in soups, stews, and mixed with buffalo meat and fat to make pemmican. The Blackfoot made juice from the berries into a dye and the Blood brewed the fruit into a remedy for stomach ache and liver trouble. Arrows, digging sticks, spears and canoe cross-pieces were made from the hard wood by Cree and Blackfoot.

Today saskatoon berries are enjoyed fresh or made into pies, muffins, etc. and the attractive fall colouration of the shrub makes it a popular ornamental.

There are twelve species of *Amelanchier* worldwide, mainly in temperate North America, but only one is native to Alberta.

The masses of white flowers, attractive fall colours, and tasty berries make the saskatoon a popular ornamental.

Adequate spring moisture produces abundant, juicy berries.

Saskatoons may grow as slender trees or compact shrubs in Alberta.

ROUND-LEAVED HAWTHORN;
GOLDEN-FRUITED HAWTHORN

Crataegus rotundifolia
Rose Family (Rosaceae)

Habitat and range: Coulees, river valleys, and open woods in the southern half of the province. Prairie and Aspen Parkland.

Flowers: In clusters at the ends of branches, showy. Petals five, white, yellow or pink, to 8 mm long. Sepals five, green, 3 – 4 mm long. Stamens five to twenty-five, yellow. Blooms from May to July.

Fruit: Red or orange-yellow berry-like pome, to 1 cm across, with many large seeds. Appears like a small apple.

Leaves: Simple, alternate, 2.5 – 5 cm across. Broad, sometimes divided into three or four triangular lobes, doubly toothed except near the base. Teeth commonly with red margins. Leaves sometimes hairy beneath, at least on the veins. Leaf stalks (petioles) often with dark red, raised glands.

Growth habit: Large, much-branched shrub or small tree 1 – 5 m tall, with a narrow crown. Usually covered with many long sharp, slender thorns, 2 – 7 cm long. Twigs with a characteristic zig-zag shape; winter buds broad, dome-shaped, shiny. Bark shreddy.

The fruit is often called "haw," hence the name hawthorn. The generic name is from the Greek *kratos* (strength) referring to the strong wood. *Rotundifolia* means round-leaved.

Although the fruit of the related black hawthorn (*C. douglasii*) was eaten occasionally by the Blackfoot, hawthorn berries and leaves contain a digitalis-like glycoside and can be toxic if consumed in large quantities. The Cree used the branches as pegs in wooden carts and various native people used the thorns as awls and fishhooks, and the strong wood for making digging sticks, clubs and implement handles.

There are three hundred or more species of *Crataegus* in the Northern Hemisphere, many of which interbreed. The other Alberta species, black hawthorn, may be distinguished from round-leaved hawthorn by its darker (nearly black) mature fruit, shorter, thicker thorns and leaves which are smooth, rather than hairy beneath. Black hawthorn is rare in Alberta and is found in open woods and rocky banks in the Waterton area and the Cypress Hills.

C. WERSHLER

Petals may be white, yellowish or pink.

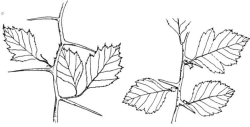

Long, slender thorns of golden-fruited hawthorn (left) contrasted with the short, thick thorns of black hawthorn.

B. ANDRUSEK

The "berries" may look tempting but they contain a toxic chemical.

SHRUBBY CINQUEFOIL
Potentilla fruticosa
Rose Family (Rosaceae)

Habitat and range: Dry slopes, open woods to Subalpine elevations. Common in the foothills and Prairies.

Flowers: Numerous; single in the leaf axils or in small, dense clusters at the ends of branches. Petals five, bright yellow, rounded, 3–10 mm long. Stamens 25–30, yellow. Sepals five, soft-hairy, tapered to a sharp point. Blooms from June to August.

Fruit: Clusters of light brown achenes 1.5–2 mm long, with long, whitish hairs.

Leaves: Pinnately compound. Leaflets, usually five per leaf, are grey-green, lighter below; silky-hairy. Leaflets narrowly oblong, entire, 5–15 mm long, tapered at each end, with margins often inrolled. Short-petioled. Brown, papery sheathing bracts (stipules) at the bases of the leaves.

Growth habit: Spreading to erect leafy shrub to 1 m tall. Much-branched with red-brown, shredding bark on mature plants. Young branches silky-hairy.

The name cinquefoil, from the French *cinq* (five), applies to the five-parted leaves. *Potentilla* comes from the Latin *potens* (powerful) because of the potent medicinal properties of some of the species and *fruticosa* is from the Latin *fruticari* (to sprout or become bushy).

The dry, shredding bark was used as tinder by Blackfoot Indians and the dried leaves can be used to make a tea. Cultivated varieties of shrubby cinquefoil are popular today as ornamentals.

There are approximately two hundred species of *Potentilla* worldwide, mostly in temperate zones of the Northern Hemisphere. Although only one shrubby *Potentilla* is native to our province, twenty-seven herbaceous species occur here.

Shrubby cinquefoil occurs in both dry areas and near lakeshores.

The masses of bright yellow flowers make shrubby cinquefoil a popular addition to the garden.

PIN CHERRY;
Bird Cherry
Prunus pensylvanica
Rose Family (Rosaceae)

Habitat and range: Dry to moist woods, clearings, coulees, hillsides, river banks. Often on dry, sandy soil. Shade-intolerant. Establishes readily after a fire. Widespread throughout the province, except the southeastern Prairie.

Flowers: In loose clusters of five to seven, on long pedicels, from a common point on the twig. Petals in fives, creamy-white, showy, 6 – 8 mm long. Stamens 30. Flowers short-lived. Blooms May – June.

Fruit: A bright red berry-like drupe, 5 – 7 mm in diameter, containing one large stone. Clusters of several fruits with long stalks attached to one point on the same twig, as contrasted to fruit spaced along a central stalk in choke cherry. Sour but edible. Ripens from August to September.

Leaves: Simple, alternate. Lance-shaped or oval, finely toothed, 3 – 10 cm long, tapering gradually to a slender, pointed tip. Light green, turning pinkish-orange to bright red in the fall. Midvein prominent below. Leaf stalks slender, 5 – 15 mm long.

Growth habit: Straight-trunked small tree to 8 m high or slender shrub on dry soils. Young bark smooth, dark red-brown; mature bark with large orange horizontal markings (lenticels).

Prunus is from the Greek *prunos* meaning plum and *pensylvanica* means from Pennsylvania in Latin. The berries are eaten by birds and were eaten raw by some Indian tribes but the green inner bark, wilted leaves, and fruit pits produce hydrocyanic acid when ingested and are poisonous. The bark of related species, and possibly pin cherry as well, was used by several British Columbian Indian tribes for decorating mats and baskets, as twine, to wrap implements, and to cover wound dressings.

There are two hundred species of *Prunus* in the temperate Northern Hemisphere and Andes Mountains of South America. Pin cherry may be distinguished from the other Alberta *Prunus* species, choke cherry, by leaf characteristics and the fruit and flower attachment to the twigs.

The flowers of pin cherry are showy but short-lived.

The brightly-coloured fruit is sour but edible.

Typical habitat of pin cherry.

CHOKE CHERRY; WILD CHERRY
Prunus virginiana
Rose Family (Rosaceae)

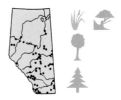

Habitat and range: Stream banks, thickets; protected, shaded areas in coulees; open woods on rich, moist soils. Common except in the far north of the province.

Flowers: Fragrant, in long, bottle brush-like clusters, 5 – 15 cm long. Flowers on short, wide-spreading pedicels, 4 – 8 mm long. Petals five, cream-coloured to white, 2 – 4 mm long. Stamens 20 – 25, yellow-tipped. Sepals five, glandular. Blooms May – June.

Fruit: Pea-sized dark red to purple-black, shiny, berry-like drupe, 8 – 10 mm long, containing a large stone. Edible.

Leaves: Dark, dull green above, lighter beneath, 6 – 10 cm long. Oblong, abruptly tapered to a short, sharp tip, with finely toothed margins. Petioles 5 – 15 mm long with one or two purple wart-like glands near the leaf base.

Growth habit: Slender shrub or small tree to 10 m tall, often with a crooked trunk and irregular crown. Branches red-brown, slender, ascending. Mature bark dark grey.

Choke cherry alludes to the sensation of choking caused by eating the sour-tasting berries. The species name *virginiana* is the Latin for "of Virginia."

The fruits are relished by birds, bears and rodents and were eaten raw and dried for use in soups, stews and pemmican by the Blackfoot. The Blackfoot and Cree are believed to have boiled the bark with other ingredients to produce a remedy for diarrhoea, and tea made from the boiled twigs was said to relieve fevers. The dried roots were chewed and placed on wounds to stop bleeding by both Blackfoot and Plains Cree, and the wood used for digging sticks, roasting skewers, arrows and tipi construction. Choke cherry berries are currently used to make wine, jellies and syrups. However the inner bark, pits and wilted leaves contain a compound which breaks down in the body to form hydrocyanic acid, and the plant has caused fatalities in children and livestock.

Several varieties of choke cherry are cultivated as ornamentals in Alberta because of their attractive berries and fall leaf colouration.

Flowers attached in clusters and gradually tapered leaves of pin cherry (left) contrasted with flowers along a central stalk and abruptly tapered leaves of choke cherry (right).

The fragrant flowers of choke cherry are grouped into long clusters.

Choke cherry berries are edible but very tart.

115

PRICKLY ROSE
Rosa acicularis
Rose Family (Rosaceae)

Habitat and range: Woods, river banks, roadsides, fields, clearings. Common throughout the province except in the southeastern Prairies.

Flowers: Flowers showy, usually occurring singly on new lateral branches. Petals usually five, light or deep pink, spreading, 2 – 3 cm long. Sepals five, leaf-like. Stamens numerous, yellow. Blooms June to August.

Fruit: Bright red or orange-red "hip" composed of hairy one-seeded fruits (achenes). Fruit pear-shaped or occasionally round, to 2 cm long. Persistent over winter.

Leaves: Alternate, pinnately compound, with 3 – 7 elliptical to oval leaflets, 2.5 – 4 cm long. Leaf base obtuse or rounded, margins coarsely toothed. Lower surface often somewhat hairy. Stipules hairy, covered with tiny glands on the margins.

Growth habit: Bushy shrub to 2.5 m tall. Stems thick, densely prickly with straight, slender prickles of unequal length.

Flowers vary in colour from very pale pink to nearly red.

Rosehips are an excellent source of vitamin C.

Rosa is from the Latin name for the genus while *acicularis* means narrow or pointed, perhaps referring to the prickles. The popular prickly rose was declared Alberta's floral emblem in 1930. Young shoots, fruits, flowers, and leaves of rose species were eaten by certain Indian tribes and a tea brewed from the roots was used to treat diarrhoea by the Blackfoot. The branches were fashioned into arrows and the stems hollowed out to make pipe stems by certain British Columbia tribes. Prickly wild rose is occasionally grown as an ornamental in Alberta.

The prickly rose is Alberta's provincial floral emblem.

B. ANDRUSEK

COMMON WILD ROSE

Rosa woodsii
Rose Family (Rosaceae)

Habitat and range: Coulees, dry slopes, river banks, sand hills, open woods. Widespread throughout the province.

Flowers: In small clusters or, rarely, solitary. Petals five, light to dark pink (occasionally white), broad, 1.5 – 2.5 cm long. Sepals five, 1 – 2 cm long. Stamens numerous, yellow. Blooms June – July.

Fruit: Bright red or orange-red, round or pear-shaped "hips" 5 – 15 mm long, containing hairy, dry achenes.

Leaves: Pinnately compound, usually with five to nine bluntly elliptical, sharp-toothed leaflets, to 2.5 cm long, often wedge-shaped at the base. Smooth to slightly hairy, occasionally glandular beneath.

Growth habit: Attractive, bushy shrub to 1.5 m tall. Branches red-brown with few to many prickles, those prickles beneath the stipules usually longer and thicker than the stem prickles.

The species name *woodsii* alludes to the wooded habitat in which the species is sometime found. The Blackfoot and Blood tribes of Alberta removed the seeds then ate the rose hips fresh, boiled or roasted, or froze them for later use. The hips were also used in decorations on clothing and in necklaces. Certain Indian tribes are said to have believed that roses could provide some protection against ghosts and evil spirits.

Teas made from both the petals and hips (which are high in vitamins C and A, calcium, phosphorus and iron) are coming back into popularity. Common wild rose is occasionally grown as an ornamental in Alberta.

There are over one hundred species of rose native to the Northern Hemisphere. The three Alberta species tend to hybridize making identification difficult. Prairie rose (*Rosa arkansana*) is generally shorter and less branched than prickly or common wild rose, dies back to the ground in the fall and has 9 – 11 leaflets. It is found in the southern half of the province and in the Peace River country. It is more difficult to distinguish common wild rose from prickly rose. Usually the former has large, thick prickles just below the stipules (see illustration) and shorter (less than 25 mm) leaflets.

Thick thorns below the stipules in common wild rose (above), distinguished from the more densely prickled prickly rose (below).

Rose flowers were once believed to provide protection against ghosts and evil spirits.

Prairie rose is shorter and has fewer branches than common wild rose or prickly rose. The flowers are sometimes almost white, with pink veins.

Wild roses are common in many diverse habitats in the province.

WILD RED RASPBERRY
Rubus idaeus
Rose Family (Rosaceae)

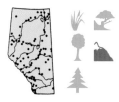

Habitat and range: Open woods, rocky slopes, cleared woodlands, banks, roadside ditches, coulees. Widespread in the province except in the southeastern Prairies.

Flowers: In small, leafy clusters. Petals five, white, oblong, 5–6 mm long. Sepals five, pale green, prickly underneath, 10–12 mm long. Stamens numerous, white with yellow tips. Blooms June–July.

Fruit: The well-known large red raspberry, composed of many tiny drupelets. Edible.

Leaves: Alternate, pinnately compound with 3–5 leaflets. Leaflets oval to lance-shaped, sharp-pointed, with doubly toothed margins and prominent veins. Pale green above; usually lighter and white-hairy below. Stipules pale green, 4–10 mm long.

Growth habit: Erect, bristly, often glandular-hairy shrub with biennial canes to 2 m tall. First year stems with broad-based prickles, often with slender bristles and glandular hairs. Bark yellowish to reddish, shredding. Thicker stems may live beyond the second year. Similar to the cultivated raspberry but not as robust.

Rubus is from the Roman name of the plant and means red; *idaeus* is from Mount Ida in Crete.

The fruit was eaten fresh and dried and also used as a dye for clothing and arrow quivers by the Blackfoot. The young suckers and twigs are edible when peeled, and the dried or fresh *unwilted* leaves (wilted leaves have caused livestock fatalities) may be used as tea. Raspberry leaf tea was used medicinally by Indian tribes as a gargle for sore throats and externally to clean wounds and act as a poultice. The roots were brewed into a tea to alleviate diarrhoea.

There are several hundred species of *Rubus*, mostly located in temperate regions of the Northern Hemisphere. The other Alberta shrub raspberry, thimbleberry (*R. parviflorus*), has larger (to 20 cm broad), coarser leaves, and larger (to 6 cm across), rose-like white flowers. The fruit is edible but is not as tasty as raspberries.

Pinnately compound leaves of wild red raspberry (left) compared to large, simple leaves of thimbleberry (right).

Flowers and leaves of thimbleberry are much larger than those of wild red raspberry.

The raspberries are borne on second-year wood.

WESTERN MOUNTAIN ASH
Sorbus scopulina
Rose Family (Rosaceae)

Habitat and range: Woods, ravines; moist, open hillsides of western and west-central Alberta.

Flowers: Numerous in dense, rounded clusters, 10–15 cm broad. Petals in fives, white, rounded to 6 mm long. Sepals five, white-hairy. Stamens numerous. Blooms in June.

Fruit: Shiny orange or red berry-like pome, 8–10 mm in diameter, with one or two seeds in each of the three to five compartments. Soft, mealy, and bitter tasting. Persistent over winter.

Leaves: Alternate, pinnately compound of nine to thirteen or more narrowly oblong leaflets, to 7 cm long, with pointed tips. Finely toothed almost to the rounded or wedge-shaped base. Dark green above, paler beneath; turning orange or red in the fall. Deciduous, green, membranous stipules at the base of each leaf.

Growth habit: Erect shrub to 4 m tall with many red-brown, much-branched stems. Bark reddish or yellowish, turning grey-red with age. Young twigs and inflorescence with long white hairs. Winter buds slightly sticky.

The common name of mountain ash evolved from the resemblance of the leaves to the leaves of the ash tree. *Sorbus* is the Latin name, which was applied to a Mediterranean species. *Scopulina* means broom-like or shrubby and is derived from the Latin *scopula* (little broom) and *-ina* (resembling). The berries, although bitter due to their high tannin content, are relished by birds and were eaten by some Indian tribes with fish or meat. The fruit should be used sparingly, however, and the seeds avoided. In Europe, various liquors are made from mountain ash (*S. aucuparia*) berries, Poland's Rowan Brandy being perhaps the most famous.

There are approximately fifty species of mountain ash in temperate and subarctic zones of North America and Eurasia. The other native mountain ash in Alberta is Sitka mountain ash (*S. sitchensis*) which may be differentiated from western mountain ash by its rusty red rather than whitish hairs on winter buds, young growth and flower clusters; fruits with a blue bloom, and leaves more rounded at the tip and base. Sitka mountain ash is rare in Alberta, having been reported only from Waterton Lakes National Park and vicinity.

The rowan tree (*S. aucuparia*), an introduced mountain ash found in Alberta, is a tree rather than a shrub and usually has 13 or more leaflets. Several species of mountain ash are grown ornamentally in Alberta.

The shrubby growth habit of western mountain ash gives the plant its specific name (*scopulina*).

Differences in leaf shape between Sitka mountain ash (above) and western mountain ash (below).

Mountain ash flowers give way to many red fruits in the fall.

The abundant berries are a favourite with waxwings in the winter.

NARROW-LEAVED MEADOWSWEET
Spiraea alba
Rose Family (Rosaceae)

Habitat and range: Moist meadows, roadsides, shores in the east-central part of the province.

Flowers: Numerous small flowers in dense, elongated, finely hairy terminal clusters. Petals five, white, 2 – 3 mm long. Sepals five, broadly triangular-shaped. Blooms in July.

Fruit: Shiny papery "pod," to 6 mm long, with an opening along one side (follicle). Usually contains four narrow seeds which are tapered at both ends.

Leaves: Simple, alternate, 4 – 6 cm long. Narrowly lance-shaped, finely toothed, and pointed at both ends. Dark green above, paler and occasionally with fine hairs on the veins beneath.

Growth habit: Slender shrub to 2 m tall, with few branches. Twigs light brown.

Narrow-leaved meadowsweet occurs in moist habitats, often along rivers or lakes.

Fruit of narrow-leaved meadowsweet.

The genus name *Spiraea* is from the Greek *speira* meaning spire or wreath and *alba* is Latin for white. Some members of this genus are very fragrant, hence the common name.

There are seventy species of *Spiraea*, mostly in temperate regions of the Northern Hemisphere. Besides narrow-leaved meadowsweet, there are two other *Spiraea* species in Alberta. Birch-leaved spiraea (*S. betulifolia*) is smaller, has a flat-topped flower cluster and broader leaves than narrow-leaved meadowsweet, and is found in woods and on slopes in the western part of the province. Pink meadowsweet (*S. densiflora*) has deep rose-pink flowers and rounder, shorter leaves. It is rare in Alberta, found only in the extreme southwest of the province.

Birch-leaved meadowsweet may be easily distinguished from narrow-leaved meadowsweet by its flat-topped flower clusters.

Pink meadowsweet is found only in the extreme southwest of the province.

125

COMMON CARAGANA;
Siberian Peatree
Caragana arborescens
Pea Family (Leguminosae)

Habitat and range: Open woods, roadsides. Introduced, naturalized, spreading from hedges or windbreaks.

Flowers: Flowers showy, bright yellow, sweet pea-like, 12–25 mm long from large buds on the previous year's wood. Calyx of five united sepals with white-hairy margins.

Fruit: Brittle, round, narrow dark brown pod, 4–5 cm long, which splits open with a loud pop to release many seeds.

Leaves: Pinnately compound with four to seven pairs of pale-green oval leaflets to 2.5 cm long. Leaves somewhat hairy when young, becoming smooth; margins entire. Short spine at the tip of the leaf. Stipules green-brown, narrow, 4 mm long, persisting as spines at the base of each petiole.

Growth habit: Spreading shrub or small tree to 4 m tall. Bark olive green to grey with horizontal markings. Leaves and flowers in clusters at nodes or leaves occurring singly.

The name caragana is the Latin form of the Mongolian name for the plant *Caragan*. The specific name *arborescens* means becoming tree-like.

Caragana is a popular ornamental shrub because it is drought-resistant, hardy and very tolerant of adverse soil conditions. Although it is often used in hedges, it is better utilized as an untrimmed specimen shrub or in windbreaks, as it has a tendency to crowd out other plants.

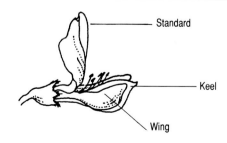

Standard

Keel

Wing

Caragana is not native to Alberta but is occasionally found as an escape from cultivation.

POISON IVY

Rhus radicans
Sumach Family (Anacardiaceae)

Habitat and range: Ravines, open woods, coulees, flood plains. Of scattered occurrence in southern and central Alberta Aspen Parkland and Prairie.

Flowers: Flowers in dense clusters in the leaf axils. Petals five, white or yellowish-white with green veins, 2–3 mm long. Sepals five, shorter and darker than petals. Stamens five. Blooms in early July.

Fruit: Dense clusters of round, white, smooth berry-like drupes, 5–6 mm wide, each containing one white, grooved seed.

Leaves: Alternate, compound, in threes. Prominently veined leaflets, 3–15 cm long on long, red petioles. Oval-shaped, pointed at the tip; irregularly toothed or entire. Shiny green, turning red in the fall.

Growth habit: Single-stemmed, erect, low-growing shrub, 10–40 cm tall. Often appearing herbaceous but woody at the base. Usually grows in patches.

The shiny, green leaves of poison ivy turn to bright red in the fall.

In eastern North America this plant has a creeping, ivy-like form, which gives it the common name of poison ivy. The generic name *Rhus* is from the Greek *rhous* (red) and likely refers to the fruit colour of some of the species or the fall leaf colour. *Radicans* means rooting, from the Latin *radix* (root) and refers to the creeping stems (stolons) which can develop roots and send up new plants, similar to strawberry runners.

This plant contains a toxic chemical in its resin canals which, on contact, produces a persistent itchy skin rash, accompanied by swelling and blisters in severe cases. Eating the leaves or fruit may be fatal. If you have been in contact with poison ivy, wash the affected parts with strong soap and water and contact your physician.

Some western U.S. Indian tribes used a mash of the leaves to cure ringworm and the plant was used by early Europeans in an attempt to cure herpes infections. There are 120 species of *Rhus* widely distributed throughout the world, except in the Arctic and Antarctic.

129

SKUNKBUSH;
Squawbush
Rhus trilobata
Sumach Family (Anacardiaceae)

Habitat and range: Banks of rivers and streams, south-facing coulee slopes, dry hillsides in Prairies south of the Red Deer River.

Flowers: Tiny, malodorous flowers in terminal clusters near the tips of branches. Flowers develop before the leaves. Petals five, yellow-green, 3 mm long. Sepals five, united. Stamens five. Flowers in mid-May.

Fruit: Round, shiny red or orange sticky-hairy berry-like drupe, 5-8 mm long. Contains one yellow-brown ribbed seed.

Leaves: Alternate, compound, to 7 cm long. In threes with the terminal leaflet fan-shaped, lobed at the tip and coarsely scalloped on the margin. The lower two leaflets are less deeply lobed and smaller; strongly wedge-shaped at the base. Dark green, paler underneath, turning purple-red in the fall. Leaves with long red petioles.

Growth habit: Rounded, much-branched shrub to 2 m tall. Stems often slightly hairy when young, becoming smooth with age. Twigs slender, with red, short hairs. Solitary or growing in clumps.

This shrub has a faint but unpleasant smell, hence the common name of skunkbush. The specific name *trilobata* means three-lobed, derived from the Greek *treis* (three) and *lobos* (lobe).

Blackfoot Indians were said to have ground the dried berries and dusted them on smallpox pustules to relieve itching.

Skunkbush may be distinguished from poison ivy (another Alberta *Rhus* species) by its much taller height, shorter more lobed leaflets, and orange-red hairy, rather than smooth white, fruits.

The unusual leaf shape of skunkbush makes it easy to recognize.

The tiny, malodorous flowers
generally appear before the leaves.

MOUNTAIN LOVER;
MOUNTAIN BOXWOOD;
False Box
Pachistima myrsinites
Bittersweet Family (Celastraceae)

Habitat and range: Coniferous forest, mountain slopes, rocky outcrops and thickets in and adjacent to Waterton Lakes National Park. Rare in Alberta.

Flowers: Small, numerous in clusters in the leaf axils or solitary. Petals four, maroon or brick-red, 1.5 mm long. Stamens four. Blooms May – June.

Fruit: Small, oval capsule, 3 – 5 mm long, containing one or two dark brown seeds with thin, white, shredded, seed coats.

Leaves: Simple, opposite, numerous; 1 – 3 cm long. Ever-green, leathery, oblong; toothed at the margin.

Growth habit: Erect or spreading, much-branched compact shrub, usually 20 – 60 cm tall. Branches brown, smooth, four-angled.

Pachistima is from the Greek *pachys* (thick) and *stigma* (stigma). The specific name is from the Greek word for myrrh *myrsine* and alludes to the pleasant scent of the flowers. Florists used this attractive plant for floral sprays to the extent that it has been all but wiped out near some large cities in the American Northwest. Where it is hardy, it is popular as an ornamental because of its evergreen foliage and compact habit. There are two species of *Pachistima* in North America; only one occurs in Alberta.

Capsule and seed detail of mountain lover.

This compact evergreen shrub is found only in the extreme southwest of the province.

ROCKY MOUNTAIN MAPLE;
Douglas Maple
Acer glabrum
Maple Family (Aceraceae)

Habitat and range: Mountain slopes, stream banks, sheltered ravines in the Rockies.

Flowers: Male and female flowers usually on separate trees. Flowers five to fifteen in clusters, drooping from the leaf axils and the ends of branches. Flowers to 8 mm broad. Petals five, small, sometimes lacking. Sepals usually five, green, prominently veined, to 4 mm long.

Fruit: A one-seeded, dry, winged fruit called a samara, 2 – 4 cm long. Fruits in pairs, wrinkled bases united and wings almost parallel. Green to pink-tinged, turning light brown in the fall.

Leaves: Simple, opposite, three to five-lobed. Smooth to occasionally sparsely glandular-hairy, thin, prominently veined, 3–10 cm across, on slim red or green petioles. Margins irregularly and doubly toothed. Dark green above, paler on the lower surface; turning dull red in the fall.

Growth habit: An attractive, much-branched shrub or small tree to 10 m tall. Young twigs green or red; mature bark smooth, red to grey.

The name Douglas maple honours David Douglas, a 19th century Scottish botanist who discovered many plant and bird species of British Columbia, the primary range of this tree. *Acer* is the Latin for maple tree and *glabrum* is the Latin for smooth or without hairs.

The Thompson Indians of B.C. drank a mixture of boiled Rocky Mountain maple bark and wood to cure nausea, and other Indian peoples used the tough, pliable wood for snowshoe frames, tipi pegs, bows, fish traps and spear handles. The bark could be used for rope and the wood was known as an excellent fuel. The seeds, twigs, and young leaves are heavily utilized by wildlife.

Rocky Mountain maple is popular as an ornamental because of its colourful fall leaves and small size.

The leaves of the Rocky Mountain Maple turn to a dull red in the fall.

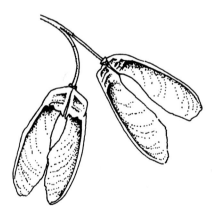

Fruit (samara) of Rocky Mountain maple.

MANITOBA MAPLE; BOX ELDER
Acer negundo
Maple Family (Aceraceae)

Habitat and range: Prefers moist soils along streams, ponds, ravines, wooded valleys. Mostly introduced, rather than native to Alberta.

Flowers: Male and female flowers on separate trees. Female flowers pale yellow-green, in open, drooping clusters. Male flowers red, in dense, drooping clusters on stalks 1 – 4 cm long. Both male and female flowers have four or five sepals, but no petals. Flowers appear with or before the leaves.

Fruit: Samara v-shaped, very wrinkled and usually woolly-hairy, 2 – 3 cm long with inward-curved tips. Red-tinged on the margins when young. Hanging from the branches till winter or spring.

Leaves: Pinnately compound leaves, 6 – 7 cm long, with three to five (sometimes seven) coarsely toothed or shallowly lobed leaflets. Terminal leaflet stalked, often three-lobed. Leaflets sharp-pointed. Light green above; grey-green below, occasionally with hairs; turning yellow in fall.

Growth habit: Tree to 12 m tall, with widely spreading branches. Bark grey-brown, smooth; becoming deeply grooved and darker on older trees. Twigs light green, often with a white bloom; sometimes hairy.

The specific name is taken from *nurgundi*, a Sanskrit and Bengali term for the chaste tree of India which has similar leaves. Some Indian tribes, among them the Alberta Cree, made maple sugar from the Manitoba maple's plentiful sap. Nowadays it is often used for shelterbelts and as an ornamental because it is hardy and fast-growing, although it is short lived. The wood is used occasionally for boxes and construction. There are one hundred and twenty-three species of maple (*Acer* genus) in the world, two of which occur in Alberta. Manitoba maple may be distinguished from Rocky Mountain maple by its compound leaves.

Female flowers (shown here) and male flowers are on separate trees.

Maple sugar can be made from the sap of the Manitoba maple.

The leaves are pinnate and do not
have the characteristic maple shape.

DEERBRUSH; SNOWBRUSH;
Sticky Laurel
Ceanothus velutinus
Buckthorn Family (Rhamnaceae)

Habitat and range: Dry woods, Montane to Subalpine shrubby slopes in Waterton Lakes National Park and vicinity. Rare in Alberta.

Flowers: Numerous, tiny but showy in dense terminal clusters or on axillary branches. Petals five, green to white, each with a hood and a long claw. Stamens and sepals five. Sweet-smelling. Blooms June – July.

Fruit: Glandular capsule, 4 – 5 mm long, separating into three compartments at maturity, each with one flattened seed.

Leaves: Alternate, simple, evergreen, persistent. Strong-smelling, oval, 4 – 8 cm long, with a rounded tip. Margins finely toothed with glandular teeth. Upper surface somewhat sticky, shiny, dark green above, paler below. Prominently three-veined from the base.

Growth habit: Spreading, round shrub to 3 m tall. Grows in thick patches. Twigs olive-green, minutely hairy to smooth, sticky when young.

Ceanothus is a Greek name for a spiny shrub of unknown origin. The specific name *velutinus* means velvety, in reference to the underside of the leaf.

Smoke from the burning branches was used by certain B.C. tribes to disinfect houses and act as an insect repellent. The leaves were brewed into a tea and the plant was used medicinally as a cough syrup, blood purifier, and to treat tuberculosis. Rubbing the flowers in the hand with water produces a soapy lather. A closely related species (*C. americanus*) was a source of tea for the Americans after the Boston Tea Party. The leaves are eaten by deer, elk, and moose.

There are forty species of *Ceanothus*; all in North America, mostly in California. Deerbrush is the only *Ceanothus* species in Alberta.

The evergreen leaves of deerbrush are leathery and prominently-veined.

ALDER-LEAVED BUCKTHORN
Rhamnus alnifolia
Buckthorn Family (Rhamnaceae)

Habitat and range: Moist ground along streams or in shady woods. In the Waterton Lakes National Park area and in northeastern Alberta.

Flowers: Flowers usually male or female and on separate plants. Flowers green yellow, 4 – 5 mm broad, single or clustered in the axils of lower leaves. Usually without petals (apetalous). Sepals five (sometimes four). Blooms in June or July.

Fruit: Reddish to blue-black berry-like drupe, 6 – 10 mm long with three seeds. Poisonous.

Leaves: Alternate. Simple. Leaf blades lance-shaped, thin, 3 – 10 cm long with six to eight prominent veins and with glandular, finely scalloped margins. Short-petioled. Stipules 3 – 6 mm long, deciduous.

Growth habit: Low, erect or spreading shrub to 2 m tall. Stems finely grey-hairy, becoming smooth and dark grey-brown with age.

Alder-leaved buckthorn has prominently-veined leaves quite similar to those of red-osier dogwood.

The genus name is from the Greek *rhamnos* (buckthorn) or the Celtic *rham* (a tuft of branches). Alnifolia means alder-like leaves, from the Latin *alnus* (alder) and *folium* (leaf). The bark, leaves and fruit contain glycosides and are strongly purgative.

There are one hundred species of buckthorn in temperate and subtropical regions; two occur in Alberta. The introduced European buckthorn (*R. catharticus*) is much taller (to 6 m tall), has spine-tipped twigs and opposite leaves. It is rare in Alberta but is occasionally seen in southern coulees.

European buckthorn has berries that are strongly purgative.

WOLF-WILLOW; SILVERBERRY

Elaeagnus commutata
Oleaster Family (Elaeagnaceae)

Habitat and range: Moist plains, ravines and slopes, coulees, stream banks. Often on gravelly or light soil as it can tolerate dry conditions. Common, particularly in southern Alberta.

Flowers: Flowers arranged in short-stalked clusters of three or four in axils or at the bases of the current year's twigs. Flowers to 15 mm long, tubular with four pointed lobes which are yellow inside and silvery outside. Stamens four; petals lacking. Strong-smelling. Blooms May – June.

Fruit: Silvery-coloured, dry, mealy, berry-like, 10 – 12 mm long; containing a large, stony, eight-grooved seed.

Leaves: Simple, alternate, wavy, numerous, silvery-green. Oblong, sharply-pointed or somewhat blunt at the tip, to 10 cm long. Sometimes with occasional rusty-coloured scales beneath. Short-petioled.

Growth habit: Erect or spreading, moderately branched shrub to 4 m tall. Young branches with tiny rusty and silvery scales, older branches grey-brown.

While the origin of the name of the silverberry is self-evident, the source of the common name wolf-willow is unknown. Perhaps it refers to the rather pungent smell of the plant in bloom. *Elaeagnus* is derived from the Greek *elaia* (olive) and *agnos* (the name of a

The seeds inside the attractive silver "berries" were used by the Blackfoot in decorative beadwork.

The yellow-tipped flowers of wolf-willow are small but have a pungent aroma.

plant with similar foliage). *Commutata*, from the Latin *commutare* (to change) supposedly refers to the leaves which are changed from green to silver-grey.

The fruits were used for food in times of famine by the Blackfoot, and also for decorative bead work by both Blackfoot and Cree. Certain B.C. tribes used the tough, fibrous bark for weaving baskets and making rope for nets, bags, clothing, fishing line, etc. There are twenty species of *Elaeagnus* in the north temperate zones of the world but the only other member of this genus in Alberta is introduced Russian olive (*E. angustifolia*). It has narrower leaves and yellowish rather than silver berries. Both wolf-willow and Russian olive are grown here as ornamentals.

Russian olive is similar to wolf-willow but has narrower, greener leaves.

Wolf-willow may occur singly or in small to large colonies.

SEA BUCKTHORN

Hippophae rhamnoides
Oleaster Family (Elaeagnaceae)

Habitat and range: An escape from cultivation. Rare in the province.

Flowers: Male and female flowers on separate plants; appearing before the leaves. Inconspicuous, small, yellow; found in clusters.

Fruit: Berry-like, orange, persistent; to 7 mm in diameter. Acidic.

Leaves: Simple, alternate. Silvery-green and scaly. Narrow, linear, 2–6 cm long. Short-petioled.

Growth habit: Bushy shrub or small tree to 5 m tall with somewhat spiny branches. The bark is scaly and light grey on young branches.

This tree is often found growing on saline shores, hence the common name sea buckthorn. The genus name *Hippophae* is from the Greek *hippophaes* for a spiny plant of unidentified origin. *Rhamnoides* is likely from the Greek *rhamnos* for buckthorn or the Celtic *rham* meaning a tuft of branches.

The sea buckthorn is native to Europe and Asia but is grown here as an ornamental because it is drought- and salt-tolerant. Both the male and female trees must be planted for the female tree to bear fruit.

The narrow leaves are somewhat reminiscent of the closely related Russian olive.

K. WILKINSON

Although grown as an ornamental, sea buckthorn is not a particularly attractive shrub.

THORNY BUFFALOBERRY; SILVER BUFFALOBERRY; Bullberry

Shepherdia argentea
Oleaster Family (Elaeagnaceae)

Habitat and range: Open woods, stream banks, north-facing slopes, coulees in southern Alberta.

Flowers: Male and female flowers on separate plants; clustered on short branches in the leaf axils. Flowers small (2 mm in diameter), yellow or brown. No petals, four sepals, eight stamens. Blooms late April to May.

Fruit: In thick clusters. Berry-like, bright red, orange or yellow, 4 – 6 mm long, containing one large seed. Edible but somewhat bitter until after a frost.

Leaves: Simple, opposite. Oblong, 2 – 5 cm long, rounded at the tip and wedge-shaped at the base. Entire with thin silvery scales on both sides.

Growth habit: Shrub to 6 m tall with wide-spreading branches. Twigs silvery-scurfy when young. Older branches brown, twisted, with thorns to 3 cm long. May form dense thickets along streams and in coulees.

The generic name honours John Shepherd, an 18th century English botanist, and the specific name *argentea* is from the Latin *argentum* meaning silver. The Blackfoot believed that buffalo relished the plant, hence the common name. The berries were eaten fresh, dried for winter use, or cooked into a sauce which was served with buffalo meat, but they were mainly considered a famine food. This species is high in a chemical called saponin and can cause severe digestive upset when consumed in quantity. Plains Indians made thongs and laces out of the bark.

Branches of thorny buffaloberry.

The berries make excellent jam but are bitter when raw and should be eaten with caution.

CANADA BUFFALOBERRY; SOOPOLALLIE; Russet Buffaloberry; Soapberry

Shepherdia canadensis
Oleaster Family (Elaeagnaceae)

Habitat and range: Shore lines, river banks; often on limestone soil. Abundant in semi-open, dry pine or spruce woods to tree-line. Widespread throughout the province except in the southeastern Prairie.

Flowers: Male and female flowers on separate plants, clustered in the leaf axils. Female flowers small (to 4 mm wide), reddish-yellow and surrounded by short, erect sepals. Male flowers brown, surrounded by four spreading to reflexed sepals, 1 – 4 mm long. Stamens eight. Both male and female flowers lack petals. Blooms May – June.

Fruit: Red or orange berry-like fruit, 4 – 6 mm long. Edible in small quantities.

Leaves: Simple, opposite, thick. Narrowly oval, 2 – 5 cm long, with a round tip and short petiole. Somewhat turned under at the margins, entire. Dark green above, silvery-scaled with rusty dots beneath.

Growth habit: Spreading to erect shrub to 3 m tall, with smooth, grey bark. The young twigs, buds and leaf undersides are dotted with tiny brown and silvery scales.

Canada buffaloberry is characteristic of Montane spruce and pine forests.

Plains Indians are said to have flavoured buffalo meat with these berries, a possible origin for the common name buffaloberry. *Canadensis* is the Latin form of Canadian. Soopolallie is Chinook Indian for soapberry, from *soop* (soap) and *olallie* (berry), and refers to the tendency of the berries to foam when beaten with water. The resulting mixture, called Indian ice cream, is relished by certain tribes. The saponin which gives the berries their foaming properties can cause digestive upset and therefore the fruit should be used in moderation. The iron-rich berries were also eaten fresh or dried and are still used by some tribes as tonics for blood disorders and relief of acne.

There are three species of buffaloberry in North America; two are native to Alberta. Canada buffaloberry differs from thorny buffaloberry in that it lacks thorns, and has green, more oval leaves compared to the narrowly oblong, grey leaves of thorny buffaloberry. Both are occasionally grown as ornamentals in Alberta.

Detail of male (left) and female (right) flowers of Canada buffaloberry.

B. ANDRUSEK

The berries of Canada buffaloberry make a foamy "Indian ice cream" when whipped with water.

DEVIL'S-CLUB
Oplopanax horridum
Ginseng Family (Araliaceae)

Habitat and range: Moist, shaded woods near streams, lake shores; often in rich soil. In north central Alberta in the Swan Hills and near Lesser Slave Lake. Also in Waterton Lakes National Park.

Flowers: Numerous, in a terminal cluster, 10 – 30 cm long. Petals five, greenish-white, 5 – 6 mm long. Sepals five. Stamens five. Blooms in June.

Fruit: Bright red, waxy, flattened berry-like drupe, 4 – 8 mm long, with two or three seeds. Inedible.

Leaves: Simple, alternate, maple-leaf shaped. Very large, 10 – 40 cm broad, with five to seven sharp-pointed lobes. Margins unevenly toothed. Prominently veined, veins prickly beneath.

Growth habit: Robust, strong-smelling shrub to 3 m tall. Stems thick, upright or trailing. Stems, leaf veins and petioles covered with sharp, yellow spines, 5 – 10 mm long.

Oplopanax originates from the Greek *hoplon* (tool or weapon) and *panax* (the name of a related large-leaved plant). The common name devil's-club and the species name *horridum* vividly describe this formidable shrub. Scratches caused by devil's-club usually become inflamed due to the toxic oils released by the plant. The plant tends to form large patches which make many areas virtually impenetrable; it made the search for a route for the Canadian Pacific Railway a gruelling undertaking north of Lake Superior and in parts of B.C.

The aromatic root was mixed with tobacco and smoked to alleviate headache by the Crow Indians of Montana. Some B.C. tribes rubbed the berries into the scalp to repel lice, treat dandruff and make the hair shiny, while the stems were used as fishhooks and lures. Charcoal from the burned plants was mixed with bear grease to make a black face paint for ceremonial occasions. There are two species of *Oplopanax*, one in North America and the other in Asia.

Leaf detail of devil's-club.

K. WILKINSON

The bright red berries are inedible.

B. ANDRUSEK

Flowers are inconspicuous.

RED-OSIER DOGWOOD
Cornus stolonifera
Dogwood Family (Cornaceae)

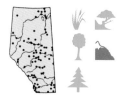

Habitat and range: Poorly drained soil, moist woods, river and stream banks; often forming thickets. Widespread throughout the province.

Flowers: Flat-topped, open, short-hairy clusters of eight to twelve tiny flowers. Petals cream-coloured or greenish-white, pointed, spreading, 2 – 3 mm long with yellow centres. Sepals four. Stamens four, white, protruding. Blooms May – July.

Fruit: White to somewhat green or blue-tinged, berry-like drupe, 6 – 9 mm long, containing one or two seeds. Bitter but edible.

Leaves: Simple; opposite. Oval, entire, 4 – 12 cm long, with prominent veins and a sharp-pointed tip. Short-petioled. Dark green above, hairy and lighter beneath. Turns to red or purple in the fall.

Growth habit: Many-stemmed, willow-like shrub to 3 m tall with smooth bark. Twigs slightly fuzzy hairy or nearly smooth. Younger branches red to yellow; older branches becoming grey. Lower branches prostrate and often rooting.

Red-osier refers to the willow-like flexible red stems and their use in basket-making (osier is another name for willow). Dogwood is said to be from "dagwood," because the wood from a coastal species of dogwood was used to make skewers or wedges called "dags" by coastal inhabitants. *Cornus* is Latin for cornel wood. *Stolonifera* is from the Greek *stolon* (a shoot) and *ferre* (to bear), and alludes to the lower branches which may take root like stolons.

The berries were considered to be a famine food by most Indian tribes but were sometimes eaten mixed with saskatoons and choke cherries. The outer bark was used by Northern Alberta tribes for dyeing and tanning hides, and the inner bark used in tobacco mixtures by Blackfoot and Cree, and boiled in a tea to reduce fever. Pipe stems were made of dogwood sticks and the wood was considered well suited for smoking and drying meat. Red-osier dogwood is often grown as an ornamental in Alberta because of its bright red bark and attractive fall leaf colour.

There are thirty species of dogwood, mainly from the north temperate regions. Of these, fifteen occur in Canada and two in

Alberta. The other Alberta dogwood, bunchberry (*C. canadensis*), is a low-growing herb less than 20 cm tall, with large, showy, white petal-like bracts.

The creamy-white flowers of red-osier dogwood occur in open clusters.

The attractive fall leaf colour and winter bark colour make this plant a popular ornamental.

153

LEATHER-LEAF
Chamaedaphne calyculata
Heath Family (Ericaceae)

Habitat and range: Muskegs, swamps, and edges of ponds; mostly north of the Athabasca River in Boreal Forest.

Flowers: In one-sided clusters. Flowers white, urn-shaped, 6–7 mm long enclosing ten stamens. Calyx five-lobed and scaly-spotted, surrounded by two hairy-margined bractlets.

Fruit: Angular, round capsule, 3–4 mm wide with compartments which split to release the seeds.

Leaves: Simple; alternate. Leathery, entire or minutely scalloped along the margins. Oblong to elliptic, 1 – 4 cm long, with a rounded to somewhat pointed tip. Scaly brown or white beneath. Short-petioled.

Growth habit: Branching shrub to 60 cm tall, with slightly hairy or scaly twigs.

The urn-shaped flowers of leather-leaf occur in one-sided clusters.

Chamaedaphne originates from the Greek *khamai* (low to the ground), and *daphne*, referring to the sweet bay or laurel members of the heath family. *Calyculata* is from the Latin *calyculatus* and refers to the bract structure below the calyx.

All Alberta members of the heath family are shrubs but many are low-growing (less than 30 cm tall) and initially appear more herbaceous than shrubby. These plants have therefore been omitted here, and will be described in a forthcoming book on wildflowers of Alberta.

Leather-leaf growth habit.

COMMON LABRADOR TEA
Ledum groenlandicum
Heath Family (Ericaceae)

Habitat and range: Muskegs, moist to wet coniferous woods, moist mountain stream banks and meadows. Usually forms the shrub understory in black spruce woods. Widespread in the mountains and the northern two-thirds of the province.

Flowers: Numerous in dense, terminal round-topped clusters. Petals five, white, oblong, narrowed at the base, 5 – 8 mm long. Flower stalks (pedicels) finely glandular-hairy. Sepals five, tooth-like, hairy, clasping the petals. Blooms June – July.

Fruit: Narrowly-oval, brown, woody, finely-hairy capsule, 5 – 7 mm long, spotted with tiny yellow glands. Capsule opens to release many tiny, elongated, winged seeds.

Leaves: Simple; alternate, entire; often persistent. Oblong to elliptic, 1 – 5 cm long, rounded at the tip, margins rolled under. Leaves leathery, green above, with dense, woolly, rusty-coloured or white hairs beneath. Short-petioled. Leaves often turn red with age. Fragrant when crushed.

Growth habit: Straggly shrub to 1 m tall, often form-

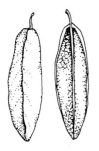

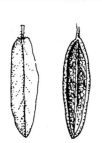

Comparison of leaves of (clockwise from left) glandular Labrador tea, northern Labrador tea and common Labrador tea.

B. ANDRUSEK

The leaves have been used in tea and medicines.

ing dense patches. Twigs and undersides of leaves densely woolly with tangled, rusty, long hairs. The leaves are crowded toward the ends of the twigs, giving the plant an unkempt appearance.

The common name is derived from the use of the leaves in tea by native people and early settlers. The generic name *Ledum* is from the Greek *ledon* (the mastick plant), a name given by the Greeks to cistus, a plant with similar leaves. The specific name is the Latin form of "from Greenland."

In addition to its use as a beverage, Labrador tea was used also as medicine for colds, sore throats, headaches, heart trouble and indigestion. Drinking the tea has been said to cause side effects ranging from dizziness and drowsiness, to diarrhoea, so caution is advised. An infusion of the leaves was applied by the Blackfoot to wounds, burns, and insect bites and Europeans used the leaves to repel rodents and noxious insects.

Another Alberta species, glandular Labrador tea (*L. glandulosum*) is toxic in large doses and has caused livestock fatalities.

There are four species of Labrador tea in North America and Eurasia. Three of these occur in Alberta. Glandular Labrador tea differs from common Labrador tea in that the leaves are pale and scaly, rather than rusty-woolly underneath. It occurs in the mountains from Banff National Park southward, but is less common in Alberta than *L. groenlandicum*. Northern Labrador tea (*L. palustre*), has smaller narrower leaves and smaller capsules, and occurs in far northern Alberta.

Fruit of Labrador tea.

Labrador tea is common in northern muskegs and in moist to wet coniferous woods elsewhere.

FALSE AZALEA;
FOOL'S HUCKLEBERRY;
Rusty-leaf Menziesia;
False Huckleberry
Menziesia ferruginea
Heath Family (Ericaceae)

Habitat and range: Moist, shady, Montane to Subalpine woods and stream banks in the Rocky Mountains.

Flowers: Flowers urn-shaped, 6 – 8 mm long, drooping in terminal clusters on slim, glandular-hairy pedicels. Petals united to form a bell or urn shape, cream to green with a pink tinge. Calyx small, saucer-shaped, with a hairy fringe. Blooms late May to July.

Fruit: Oblong, glandular, beaked capsule to 5 mm long, with four compartments containing many pointed seeds.

Leaves: Simple; alternate; in clusters at the ends of the branches. Thin, oblong, usually broadest at the tip, tapered to a short petiole. Finely toothed, smooth or sparsely hairy, 3 – 6 cm long. Pale green with long, often glandular hairs; paler and usually glandular-hairy beneath. Leaves turn orange or bright red in the fall.

Growth habit: Much-branched, spreading shrub to 2.5 m tall, with grey-brown or reddish, shreddy bark. Young twigs glandular-hairy. Unkempt-looking because of the sparse leaves.

The flowers are similar to those of huckleberry (*Vaccinium* spp.) plants, hence the common name fool's huckleberry. *Menziesia* honours Archibald Menzies, a physician and naturalist who accompanied Captain Vancouver on expeditions. *Ferruginea* is from the Latin *ferrugineus* meaning rusty-red and describes the glands on the branches, calyx and occasionally leaves of the plant.

The children of some B.C. Indian tribes are said to have sucked nectar from the flowers although the shrub contains toxic resins and is poisonous to livestock. There are six or seven species of *Menziesia* in North America and Japan but only one in Alberta.

Fruit of false azalea.

The leaves are mainly at the ends of the branches.

The urn-shaped flowers
may be cream-coloured
to pinkish.

ROCKY MOUNTAIN RHODODENDRON;
White-flowered Rhododendron
Rhododendron albiflorum
Heath Family (Ericaceae)

Habitat and range: Mainly in moist Subalpine forest. Along shaded stream banks in the Rocky Mountains and foothills, usually on acid soil.

Flowers: Showy, in nodding clusters of two or three in the leaf axils, and attached directly to the stem. Petals white or greenish-white, five-lobed, to two cm wide, in flower heads. Sepals large, pale green, stiffly glandular-hairy, forming a five-lobed calyx. Stamens ten, pale yellow, thickly hairy at their bases. Pedicels glandular-hairy. Stigma yellow, attached to a green ovary. Blooms in July.

Fruit: Oval, woody, grooved, glandular-hairy capsule, 5 – 8 mm long, with wing-margined seeds.

Leaves: Alternate or in whorls. Deciduous, 2 – 7 cm long, lance-shaped with a broad tip, tapered at both ends. Dark green, somewhat shiny above with rusty-coloured hairs, paler below. Turning orange or red in fall. Margins entire or wavy.

Growth habit: Thicket-forming shrub to 1 m. Young branches yellow green, with red hairs. Young leaves and calyx also red-hairy.

The flowers of Rocky Mountain rhododendron are large and showy.

The shrub adds colour to moist Subalpine forests.

Rhododendron is from the Greek *rhodon* (rose) and *dendron* (tree) while *albiflorum* means white-flowered in Latin. Certain B.C. tribes used the plant as a perfume and boiled the bark into a tea to alleviate upset stomach, although it contains toxic resins.

There are several hundred species of *Rhododendron*, mostly in S.E. Asia, with some in North America and Europe. Many are very showy and are cultivated as ornamentals. The only other Alberta rhododendron, Lapland rose-bay (*R. lapponicum*), has purple flowers in a terminal cluster, and leathery, dark green leaves which have brown scales beneath. It is found on moist, Subalpine slopes in mountain ranges southeast of Jasper and at Sunset Pass in Banff National Park, and is rare in Alberta.

The beautiful pink flowers of Lapland rose-bay are very similar to azaleas.

Fruit of Rocky Mountain rhododendron.

TALL BILBERRY;
MOUNTAIN HUCKLEBERRY
Vaccinium membranaceum
Heath Family (Ericaceae)

Habitat and range: Moist, Montane and Subalpine woods. Found in shaded forest and in cleared areas in the Rocky Mountains, northern foothills and along the Athabasca River.

Flowers: Urn-shaped, 5 – 6 mm long, solitary on short pedicels. Petals four to five-lobed, yellow-green or pinkish. Stamens eight to ten. Blooms in June.

Fruit: Purple to black berry, 4 – 10 mm wide with many seeds. Shiny, lacking the blueberry's characteristic white bloom. Edible and juicy.

Leaves: Simple; alternate. Oval to elliptic, 1.5 – 5 cm long. Finely toothed, smooth, tapered to a point and rounded or acute at the base. Paler beneath. Turning red in the fall.

Growth habit: Widely branching shrub, growing to 1 m tall. Young twigs somewhat angled, yellow-green; smooth. Older bark grey and shredding.

The common name bilberry is derived from the Scandinavian name for the plant, while huckleberry is a corruption of the English whortleberry. *Vaccinium* is the Latin name for blueberry, and *membranaceum* describes the thin leaves.

The very tasty berries were eaten fresh or dried by the Blackfoot and other Alberta tribes, and are used today to make pies, jams, and jellies. Certain B.C. tribes mashed the berries to make purple dye for basket materials. Both the berries and leaves can be used to make a tea.

There are approximately 150 species of blueberries in cool and mountainous regions of the world. There are eight species of *Vaccinium* in Alberta. Those under 30 cm tall will be described in the second volume of this series.

The large, juicy berries make excellent jam and pies.

Urn-shaped flowers of tall bilberry.

CANADA BLUEBERRY;
Velvet-Leaf Blueberry
Vaccinium myrtilloides
Heath Family (Ericaceae)

Habitat and range: Jack pine forests, dry muskegs. Often on sandy soils. Widespread in the northern half of the province.

Flowers: Urn-shaped, pinkish to greenish-white, in dense clusters. Petals joined to form a five-lobed corolla, 4 – 5 mm long. Calyx lobes five, broadly triangular.

Fruit: Pale blue berry, 4 – 8 mm in diameter, with a white bloom. Occurs in clusters. Edible and sweet.

Leaves: Simple; alternate. Oblong, 1 – 4 cm long, tapering to a sharp point. Bright green above, lighter and softly hairy beneath, particularly along the midvein. Margins entire. Short-petioled.

Growth habit: Low, much-branched shrub to 40 cm tall with densely hairy young twigs. Usually grows in dense patches.

The species name *myrtilloides* means "like the myrtle plant" and refers to the leaf appearance. Blueberries of various species were eaten fresh or dried in cakes by Alberta Indians and the berries

Blueberries are tasty eaten fresh or in pies.

were also made into medicinal syrup which was used to treat vomiting and diseases of the lung. Both the leaves and fruits are used to make blueberry tea.

Bog blueberry (*V. uliginosum*) differs from Canada blueberry by having prominently veined leaves which are broadest at the upper end and rounded at the tip rather than pointed. It is uncommon in Alberta and is found in Boreal Forest muskegs and on Subalpine slopes. Tall huckleberry (*V. ovalifolium*) is usually taller (to 1.5 m) than the previous two species, has solitary pinkish flowers, oval-shaped leaves, and dark blue berries with a whitish, waxy coating. It is rare in Alberta, and is found only in the Northern Rockies.

Differences in leaf shape between bog blueberry (above) and tall huckleberry (below).

Canada blueberry is common in jack pine forests.

Bog blueberry (shown here) has more rounded leaves than Canada blueberry.

FLY HONEYSUCKLE
Lonicera caerulea var. *villosa*
Honeysuckle Family (Caprifoliaceae)

Habitat and range: Swamps, muskegs and stream banks in northeastern and north central Boreal Forest.

Flowers: Flowers in pairs on short stalks from the leaf axils. Petals yellow, united to form a five-lobed, often hairy, tubular corolla, 8–15 mm long. There is a small projection at the base of the corolla which contains a nectar supply. The flowers are enclosed at the base by narrow, green bracts. Blooms June – July.

Fruit: Edible, blue-black berry, to 1 cm long, with a blue bloom. Contains many seeds.

Leaves: Simple; opposite. Oblong, 2–6 cm long, with a rounded tip and entire margins. Hairy beneath and sometimes hairy above. Short-petioled.

Growth habit: Low-growing shrub to 1.5 m tall with ascending branches. Young stems usually finely-hairy.

Honeysuckle refers to the nectar-containing corolla of this genus. *Lonicera* honours Adam Lonitzer, a 16th century German botanist. *Caerulea* is Latin for sky blue, likely referring to the bloom on the berries.

   There are approximately 150 species of Honeysuckle, mostly in temperate and subtropical regions of the Northern Hemisphere. Five species occur in Alberta, of which four are shrubs and one is a twining herbaceous perennial. Red twinberry (*L. utahensis*) has pale yellow flowers and red berries in pairs and is rare in Alberta; identified only from moist woods and slopes in southwestern Alberta. Bracted honeysuckle (*L. involucrata*) and Tartarian honeysuckle (*L. tartarica*) are described on pages 168 and 170.

The flowers of fly honeysuckle are in pairs.

B. ANDRUSEK

Red twinberry occurs only in the vicinity of Waterton Lakes National Park and the Crowsnest Pass, where it is quite common.

C. WERSHLER

BRACTED HONEYSUCKLE; BLACK TWINBERRY

Lonicera involucrata
Honeysuckle Family (Caprifoliaceae)

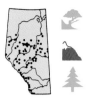

Habitat and range: Semi-open woods; rocky slopes. Widespread in moist Montane and Subalpine forests and central Alberta Boreal Forest.

Flowers: Paired in leaf axils on stalks 2 – 4 cm long. Corolla yellow, sometimes with a red tinge, 10 – 14 mm long, glandular-hairy, tube-like with five lobes at the tip. Nectary pouch at the base. Stamens numerous, yellow. Stigma greenish, protruding from the tip of the flower. Green to dark purple, leafy, spreading bracts, 1 – 2 cm long, extending from the base of the flower.

Fruit: Berries in pairs. Shiny, dark purple-black, 8 – 10 mm in diameter. Surrounded by the persistent, often reflexed, bracts. Believed poisonous.

Leaves: Simple, opposite. Bright green, oval-shaped, to 15 cm long with an abruptly pointed tip, wedge-shaped at base. More or less hairy, especially underneath along the veins. Midvein prominent. Short-petioled.

Growth habit: Attractive erect shrub to 3 m tall. Young twigs four-angled. Mature bark light brown, shredding.

Involucrata refers to the involucral bracts which surround the flowers.

The berries are inedible and believed poisonous to humans but are said to be a favourite food of bears. The Haida Indians of B.C. supposedly rubbed the berries into the scalp to prevent hair from turning grey, and the juice from the crushed berries was used as a purple dye by several Indian tribes.

The bracts that surround the flowers, and later fruits, of this honeysuckle give it its common name.

The paired flowers are yellow, or occasionally tinged with red.

TARTARIAN HONEYSUCKLE

Lonicera tartarica
Honeysuckle Family (Caprifoliaceae)

Habitat and range: Introduced in river valleys, woodlands and moist sunny locations. An escape from cultivation.

Flowers: Numerous. Paired in clusters at the ends of branches. Narrowly tubular, five-lobed, bright to pale rose-pink or nearly white, darker underneath, 7 – 18 mm long. Usually with a noticeable pouch at the base. Stamens yellow-tipped. Stigma green.

Fruit: Red, orange or yellow berries 6 – 7 mm long, united at the base.

Leaves: Simple; opposite. Dark green, lighter beneath. Oval, to 6 cm long, gradually tapered to a pointed tip. Short-petioled. Stipules minute, leaf-like.

Growth habit: Bushy, much-branched shrub to 3 m tall with a faint pleasant aroma. Bark becomes pale grey, somewhat shredding with age. Branches slender, becoming hollow.

The specific name *tartarica* refers to the plant's origins in central Asia. It is popular for ornamental plantings and hedges, as it is hardy, and insect- and disease-resistant.

Tartarian honeysuckle is not native to Alberta, but is sometimes found as a garden escape.

The berries are usually red but may also be yellow or orange.

ELDERBERRY

Sambucus racemosa
Honeysuckle Family (Caprifoliaceae)

Habitat and range: Moist woods, stream banks, clearings. Mainly in the mountains but also found in north central Alberta and the Cypress Hills.

Flowers: Numerous, crowded, in rounded or cone-shaped clusters, 4 – 10 cm long. Petals creamy-white, united to form a long tube, lobed at the tip. Stamens five. Blooms May – July.

Fruit: Round, purple black (var. *melanocarpa*) or bright red occasionally yellow or white drupes (var. *pubens*), 5 – 6 mm wide, in dense clusters. Many seeded. Bitter and likely poisonous raw.

Leaves: Pinnately compound with five to seven leaflets. Leaflets lance-shaped to elliptic, sharp-pointed, sharply toothed, 4 – 16 cm long. Lower leaves often lobed. Leaves sometimes stiffly-hairy below. Strong-smelling. Small, thickened, glandular stipules which are soon deciduous.

Growth habit: Bushy shrub to 2.5 m tall, often forming large clumps. Straggly-looking due to persistent dead stems from the previous year's growth. Twigs often with a pale green or white bloom. Stems have a wide, soft, white pith.

C. WERSHLER

Elderberry occurs in moist woods and clearings.

The berries, which may be black or red, are likely poisonous.

Sambucus is from the Greek *sambouké*, a musical instrument like a harp, which was made from elder wood. *Racemosa* means consisting of racemes (see glossary) and refers to the inflorescence type which appears to be composed of compound racemes. The variety with black berries is known as black elderberry; that with red berries as red elderberry.

The berries are favoured by birds and bears but the red-berried variety is strongly purgative, and should not be eaten raw by humans. The roots, bark and leaves are poisonous to people and livestock. Certain Indian tribes removed the poisonous pith from the centre to make flutes, blowguns, whistles and straws. After the pith is removed, however, the stem must be thoroughly dried as children have been poisoned by placing the fresh stems in their mouths. Elderberry wine, made from related species, is well known. The flowers of European species were used for tea, cooking, and in a syrup for sore throats. Flowering branches of elderberry were hung in closets to deter rodents and insects and the shrubs were planted in ancient times to keep away evil spirits and lightning. Red elderberry is grown ornamentally in Alberta.

There are twenty species of elderberry in temperate regions and mountainous areas of the tropics; three in Canada, and one in Alberta.

BUCKBRUSH;
WESTERN SNOWBERRY;
Wolfberry
Symphoricarpos occidentalis
Honeysuckle Family (Caprifoliaceae)

Habitat and range: Dry open woodland, river valleys, open hillsides, coulees, ravines. Widespread in Prairies and Aspen Parkland.

Flowers: In small terminal or axillary clusters. Flowers pink-white, urn-shaped 4 – 10 mm long with four or five lobes at the tips. White-hairy inside. Sepals five, red-tinged, united. Stamens four or five, usually protruding from the flower. Style hairy, 4 – 8 mm long. Blooms June – July.

Fruit: Greenish-white berry-like drupe, 6 – 10 mm long, that turns purplish in the autumn. Usually in dense clusters. Often persistent over winter. Believed poisonous.

Leaves: Simple; opposite. Grey-green, occasionally with a purple tinge, lighter below. Thick, oblong, entire or often wavy-toothed or occasionally lobed, 3 – 6 cm long. Smooth above; usually slightly hairy below, especially along main veins.

Growth habit: Erect, much-branched shrub to 1 m which suckers readily and forms dense thickets. Young twigs pale green to light red-brown, older bark grey-brown, shredding.

Symphoricarpos is derived from the Greek *syn* (together), *phorein* (to bear) and *karpos* (fruit) referring to the closely bunched fruits. *Occidentalis* is derived from the Latin for "western."

The leaves and inner bark were steeped in water to make an infusion for sore eyes by the Blackfoot and Cree, and the liquid from the boiled berries was given to horses as a diuretic. The twigs were made into arrow shafts and pipe stems, and tied together to make brooms.

There are ten species of *Symphoricarpos* in the world, one in China, the rest in North America. Thin-leaved snowberry (*S. albus*), the other Alberta species, closely resembles buckbrush but occurs in more wooded habitats. It has the stamens usually included within the flower and a shorter, smooth style (3 mm long or less). It is also a less robust, less branched plant and the berries remain whitish, rather than turning purplish with age.

The closely-bunched fruits of buckbrush give the plant its generic name.

The leaves of buckbrush are occasionally wavy-toothed or lobed.

The berries of thin-leaved snowberry remain white or turn yellowish with age.

LOW-BUSH CRANBERRY;
Mooseberry; Squawberry; Squashberry
Viburnum edule
Honeysuckle Family (Caprifoliaceae)

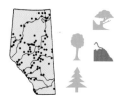

Habitat and range: Moist woods, stream banks, swamps. Widespread throughout, except in the southeastern Prairie.

Flowers: Flowers in small, rounded terminal clusters, 1 – 4 cm across on short axillary shoots. Petals white, united with five lobes. Calyx five-toothed, red-tinged. Stamens five. Blooms June – July.

Fruit: Light red or orange berry-like drupes 8 – 10 mm long in small clusters from leaf nodes. "Berries" strongly scented, with one large, flattened stone inside. Edible and juicy but tart.

Leaves: Simple; opposite. Oval, irregularly toothed, usually shallowly three-lobed, 6 – 12 cm long. Often crinkly and more or less hairy beneath, especially along the main veins. Dark green, turning red or purple in the fall.

Growth habit: Much-branched shrub to 2.5 m tall. Leaf and flower stalks, and leaf blades often with small, inconspicuous glands. Younger bark smooth, reddish, turning grey with age.

C. WALLIS

Bush cranberries make excellent jams and jellies.

176

Viburnum is the Latin name for the wayfaring-tree of Eurasia; *edule* means edible. The berries were eaten fresh or cooked by Indian tribes and some made pipe stems out of the hollowed out branches. Squawberries were highly prized by Coastal Indians and were given as gifts, as well as being eaten at feasts. The bark was sometimes used in tobacco mixtures. Nowadays bush cranberries are valued for jams and jellies. True cranberries, the source of the large, plump berries which appear traditionally at Christmas turkey dinners, actually belong to the genus *oxycoccus*, and are low-growing members of the heath family.

There are approximately 150 species of *Viburnum*, mostly in temperate regions or mountainous tropics. The other native Alberta *Viburnum* species is the high-bush cranberry (see following page) which may be distinguished from low-bush cranberry by its more deeply lobed leaves and flowers of two types.

The flowers of low-bush cranberry occur in rounded, terminal clusters.

HIGH-BUSH CRANBERRY;
Pembina
Viburnum opulus
Honeysuckle Family (Caprifoliaceae)

Habitat and range: Poplar groves, river valleys, open moist woods. Of scattered occurrence in Aspen Parkland and Boreal Forest.

Flowers: Two types of white flowers in a round-topped cluster, 5 – 15 cm across. Outer flowers larger, 1 – 2 cm broad, sterile. Both types composed of five united petals. Inner flowers smaller, 3 – 4 mm broad, with protruding stamens. Blooms May – June.

Fruit: Orange to red berry-like drupes, 8 – 10 mm in diameter, in drooping terminal clusters. "Berries" contain one stony seed. Juicy but acidic.

Leaves: Simple; opposite. Deeply three-lobed with long, pointed, spreading lobes; irregularly toothed. Smooth or stiffly hairy, 6 – 12 cm long. Deep green above, lighter beneath; turning red in the fall. Petioles reddish, to 2 cm long. Stipules up to 6 mm long, narrow, often glandular at the tips.

Growth habit: Shrub or small tree to 4 m tall, with smooth, grey bark.

Opulus means wealthy, and possibly refers to the abundant leaves or berries.

The berries were used by certain Indian tribes in making pemmican and the bark has been used as a diuretic, a sedative, and to treat septic poisoning during childbirth. Bush cranberries are popular today in jams, jellies and beverages, and are grown ornamentally for their attractive flower clusters and fall colouration.

High-bush cranberry
has two distinct types of
flowers. The larger,
showy, outer flowers are
sterile.

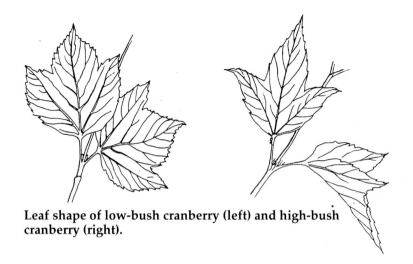

Leaf shape of low-bush cranberry (left) and high-bush cranberry (right).

C. WERSHLER

The attractive fall colours make high-bush cranberry a valued ornamental.

SAGEBRUSH;
Hoary Sagebrush; Silver Sagebrush
Artemisia cana
Composite Family (Compositae)

Habitat and range: Dry hillsides, badlands, coulees, on light, well-drained soils. Found in Prairies in the southern half of the province.

Flowers: Flowers small, yellow; in narrow, leafy clusters. Petals lacking. Thin, grey-green hairy bracts surround the flowers. Blooms July – August.

Fruit: Smooth brown achene, 1–2 mm long, spotted with yellow glands.

Leaves: Alternate. Linear to lance-shaped, 1–5 cm long. Entire or occasionally with one or two lobes at the tip. Covered with soft, silvery hairs on both sides.

Growth habit: Much-branched, often twisted shrub to 1.5 m tall. Young twigs with soft, silvery hairs. Older bark grey, shredding. Aromatic.

The name *Artemisia* honours Artemis, the Greek goddess of the hunt. *Cana* is from the Latin *canus* meaning grey-white, referring to the silky hairs covering the plant.

The Blackfoot used sagebrush to treat babies' rashes, rheumatism, adult stomach trouble, as horse medicine, and as a ceremonial plant. The leaves are said to have been chewed to relieve thirst and bloating, although many *Artemisia* species produce oils which are toxic if ingested in large amounts. Big Sagebrush (*A. tridentata*) has three tiny lobes on its wedge-shaped leaves and is found in Alberta only in Waterton Lakes National Park and the Upper Castle River Valley. It was used as a fumigant, disinfectant and insect repellent because of its strong odour.

The bark, and possibly roots, were woven into baskets, mats and saddle blankets, and the wood was used as fuel.

There are more than one hundred species of *Artemisia* in the Northern Hemisphere and South America; fifteen occur in Alberta. Most Alberta species are herbaceous.

Sagebrush growing along the Red Deer River.

K. WILKINSON

B. ANDRUSEK

Sagebrush grows in dry Prairie habitats.

Leaves of sagebrush (left) and big sage-brush (below).

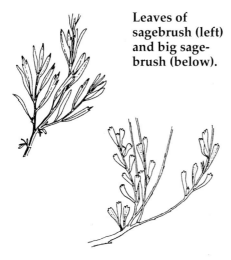

B. ANDRUSEK

Silvery leaves are characteristic of sagebrush and several other Alberta sages.

RABBIT BRUSH

Chrysothamnus nauseosus
Composite Family (Compositae)

Habitat and range: Badlands, eroded hillsides, saline clay flats. Very dry, open Prairies in southeastern Alberta. Uncommon.

Flowers: Numerous flower heads in dense, terminal clusters. Flowers bright yellow, tubular, to 10 mm long. Surrounded by several overlapping, hairy bracts of various lengths. Blooms July – August.

Fruit: Slender, hairy achene to 5 mm long, with a tuft of numerous, white, thin bristles.

Leaves: Alternate, very narrowly linear, 2 – 7 cm long; attached directly to the stem. Pointed and spread outward, entire. Pale grey-green, often covered with white, woolly hairs. Midvein grooved.

Growth habit: Bushy, low, leafy shrub to 2 m tall from a woody base. Stems and thin, wiry twigs covered with white, felty hairs. Grows in large clumps. Strong-smelling.

The common name indicates that it is a common winter browse of jack rabbits. *Chrysothamnus* means golden-crowned and refers to the conspicuous yellow flowers, while *nauseosus* refers to the strong smell. Indian tribes used the branches to smoke hides, the leaves and twigs as an insect repellent on horses, and the fruiting heads to stuff mattresses. Rabbit brush is an invader species on dry, overgrazed land and is toxic but unpalatable to livestock. There are twelve species of *Chrysothamnus*, all in western North America, but only one in Alberta.

Although the flowers are attractive, the plant has a strong, unpleasant smell.

Glossary

ACHENE   Dry, one-seeded fruit which remains closed at maturity.

ACUTE   Sharp-pointed; usually referring to the tip of a leaf or petal.

ALKALOID   Nitrogen-containing organic compound produced by some types of plants. Often poisonous.

APPRESSED   Flattened and overlapping; for example, cedar leaves.

ARIL   A fleshy, often brightly-coloured thickening of the seed coat; found in yews.

AWN   A slender bristle; found occasionally on bracts between cone scales.

AXIL   The angle formed where a leaf or branch is attached to the stem. Clusters of leaves or flowers occasionally arise from this point.

BIENNIAL   A plant which takes two years to complete its life cycle and die; for example, raspberry.

BOG   Acidic, peaty wetlands with a high water table. Usually dominated by black spruce and *Sphagnum* moss.

BRACT   A small, modified leaf associated with, but not part of, the flower; in conifers, projections attached to the central stalk of the cone.

BUTTRESSED   Flared at the base for additional support; for example, trunks of cedar trees.

CALYX   Part of the flower usually surrounding the petals. Composed of sepals.

CAPSULE   A type of fruit which contains more than one compartment, and splits open to release the seeds.

CATKIN   A cluster of small flowers, usually of one sex, which lacks petals but usually has surrounding bracts. Found on willows, poplars, alders and birches..

COMMUNITY (PLANT)   All the plants inhabiting a common environment and interacting with one another.

COMPOUND LEAF   A leaf composed of two or more distinct leaflets; for example, mountain ash.

CONIFER   A tree or shrub which bears its reproductive organs in cones.

CONTIGUOUS   Adjacent, close; refers here to dense forest growth as opposed to scattered clumps of trees above the tree-line.

COROLLA   The part of the flower composed of petals.

COULEE   Dry, often steep-sided valley common in the southeastern prairies of the province.

CROWN   The leafy top of a tree; its shape is often useful in identification.

DECIDUOUS   Falling off at the end of the growing season. In Alberta, deciduous trees and shrubs lose their leaves prior to winter.

DIOECIOUS   With male and female reproductive structures found on separate plants.

DRUPE   A fleshy fruit containing a hard, inner "stone"; for example, choke cherry.

ENTIRE   With smooth margins, referring here to leaves.

FOLLICLE   A dry fruit which is composed of only one compartment and splits open along one side to release the seeds; for example, narrow-leaved meadowsweet.

FRUIT   The ripe ovary with enclosed seeds.

GENUS (pl. GENERA)   A taxonomic group between family and species; includes one or more species with certain characteristics in common.

GLAUCOUS   With a fine, waxy, (usually white) coating which may be rubbed off; often found on berries, leaves, or twigs.

HERBACEOUS   Referring to a non-woody annual, biennial or perennial plant whose stems die back to the ground at the end of a growing season.

INDIGENOUS   Originating in or native to a country.

INFLORESCENCE   Arrangement of flowers on a plant stem.

KRUMMHOLZ   Scattered clumps of stunted, bushy trees and shrubs in Upper Subalpine and Alpine zones near tree-line.

LEADER   The tip of a tree.

LENTICEL   Small, raised spots or dots on the bark and twigs of some trees and shrubs, such as birches, which have tiny openings that allow gas exchange with the atmosphere.

MONOECIOUS   With male and female reproductive structures that are on separate flowers but on the same plant.

MUSKEG   Poorly drained wooded peatlands characterized by black spruce and *Sphagnum* moss. Found in the northern half of the province.

NECTARY   A structure that secretes nectar, usually attached to a flower.

NUT   A hard, dry one-seeded fruit which does not split open at maturity. Larger and with a firmer wall than an achene.

NUTLET   A small nut.

PEDICEL   The stalk of a single flower in a flower cluster. For example, each choke cherry flower is attached to the central stalk by a pedicel.

PETIOLE   The stalk of a leaf.

PINNATE (leaf)   Compound with leaflets arranged on each side of a central stalk.

POLLEN   Tiny grains produced by the male reproductive organs of a plant, which are transferred to the female organ for fertilization.

POME   A type of fruit with a core and usually several seeds; for example, apple.

RACEME   An elongated flower cluster with flowers attached to a central stalk by pedicels nearly equal in length; for example, choke cherry.

REFLEXED   Bent backwards.

REVOLUTE   Turned under; with margins rolled under; for example, leaves of Labrador tea.

RHIZOMES   Creeping underground stems which can develop roots and send up new shoots; for example, quack grass.

RIVERINE   Moist habitats along river banks.

SAMARA   A dry, usually one-seeded fruit with prominent wings; for example, Manitoba maple.

SEPALS   Leaf-like, usually green, appendages which surround the petals. Collectively the sepals make up the calyx. When petals are missing, the sepals are sometimes coloured like petals.

SHRUB   A low-growing woody perennial with two or more main stems.

SPECIES   A kind of organism; subdivision of a genus.

STAMEN   The male reproductive structure of a flower which produces the pollen; composed of anther and filament.

STIGMA   The part of the female reproductive organ of a flower which receives pollen.

STIPULES   Paired leaf-like appendages found at the base of the leaves in some plants.

STOLONS   Creeping above-ground stems, capable of sending up new plants.

STOMATA   (singular *stoma*) Minute openings in the surface of stems and leaves for gas exchange.

STYLE   The slender stalk connecting the stigma to the ovary in the female reproductive organ of a flower.

TREE   A perennial plant with a single, thick woody main stem.

TREE-LINE   The limit of contiguous tree cover in the mountains. Above tree-line, trees may occur in occasional scattered, small clumps.

TRUNCATE   With the tip or base appearing as though cut straight off; here, referring to leaves.

UTRICLE   A small, thin-walled, one-seeded, somewhat inflated fruit.

Selected Bibliography

Note: * denotes references most suitable for those with some botanical training.

Angier, Bradford. 1974. *Field guide to edible wild plants.* Stackpole Books.

Brockman, C.F. 1979. *Trees of North America: a guide to field identification.* Golden Press.

Clark, Lewis J. 1976. *Wild flowers of the Pacific Northwest.* Gray's Publishing Ltd.

Gibbons, E. & G. Tucker. 1979. *Euell Gibbon's handbook of edible wild plants.* Donning Co., Publ.

Hellson, J.C. & M. Gadd. 1974. *Ethnobotany of the Blackfoot Indians.* National Museum of Man. Canadian Ethnology Service Paper No. 19.

Hitchcock, C.C., A. Cronquist, M. Ownbey & J.W. Thompson. 1977. *Vascular plants of the Pacific Northwest.* Parts 1-5. University of Washington Press.*

Hosie, R.C. 1979. *Native trees of Canada.* Fitzhenry and Whiteside Ltd., Publ.

Johnston, A. 1982. *Plants and the Blackfoot.* Occasional Paper No.15. Lethbridge Historical Society.

Kerik, Joan. 1985. *Living with the land: use of plants by the native people of Alberta.* Alberta Culture. Provincial Museum of Alberta Travelling Exhibits Program.

Kingsbury, J.M. 1964. *Poisonous plants of the United States and Canada.* Prentice-Hall, Inc.

Lampe, Kenneth E. 1985. *American Medical Association handbook of poisonous and injurious plants.* American Medical Association, Chicago.

Moss, E.H. 1983. 2nd Ed., revised by J.G. Packer. *Flora of Alberta.* University of Toronto Press.*

Packer, J.G. & C.E. Bradley. 1984. *A checklist of the rare vascular plants in Alberta.* Provincial Museum of Alberta Natural History Occasional Paper No. 5.

Stearns, W.T. 1966. *Botanical Latin.* Thomas Nelson and Sons (Canada) Ltd.*

Strong, W.L. and K.R. Leggat. 1981. *Ecoregions of Alberta.* Resource Evaluation and Planning Division, Alberta Energy and Natural Resources.

Turner, N.J. 1978. *Food Plants of British Columbia Indians. Part 2/Interior Peoples.* British Columbia Provincial Museum Handbook No. 36.

Turner, N.J. 1979. *Plants in British Columbia Indian technology*. British Columbia Provincial Museum Handbook No. 38.

Turner, N.J. 1982. *Food Plants of British Columbia Indians. Part 1/Coastal Peoples*. British Columbia Provincial Museum Handbook No. 34.

Turner, N.J. & A.F. Szczawinski. 1978. *Wild coffee and tea substitutes of Canada*. National Museum of Natural Sciences.

Turner, N.J. & A.F. Szczawinski. 1979. *Edible wild fruits and nuts of Canada*. National Museum of Natural Sciences.

Weiner, M.A. 1972. *Earth medicine — earth foods*. Collier, Macmillan, Ltd.

Index

About the Author

Kathleen E. Wilkinson has an M.Sc. from the University of Calgary in plant ecology, and has won several awards and scholarships for her work in the field of plant sciences. She is a member of the International Wildlife Federation, the Canadian Society of Environmental Biologists, the Canadian Nature Federation, the Alberta Native Plant Council and the Alberta Wilderness Association. Currently a freelance vegetation consultant, she lives in Calgary with her husband and son, where hiking, natural history, music and photography are among her interests.